Dear Chad,

Our Paths Crossed And I Felt I Needed To Pass This Book On..... To You.

CHERISH IT!

SERITA

THE NECTAR OF CHANTING

SIDDHA MEDITATION ASHRAMS

PUBLISHED BY SYDA FOUNDATION
SOUTH FALLSBURG, NEW YORK

First edition published 1975. Third edition 1984.

Printed in the United States of America.
Published by SYDA Foundation.
P.O. Box 600, South Fallsburg, New York 12779.
ISBN: 0-914602-16-0 LCCN: 78-68854

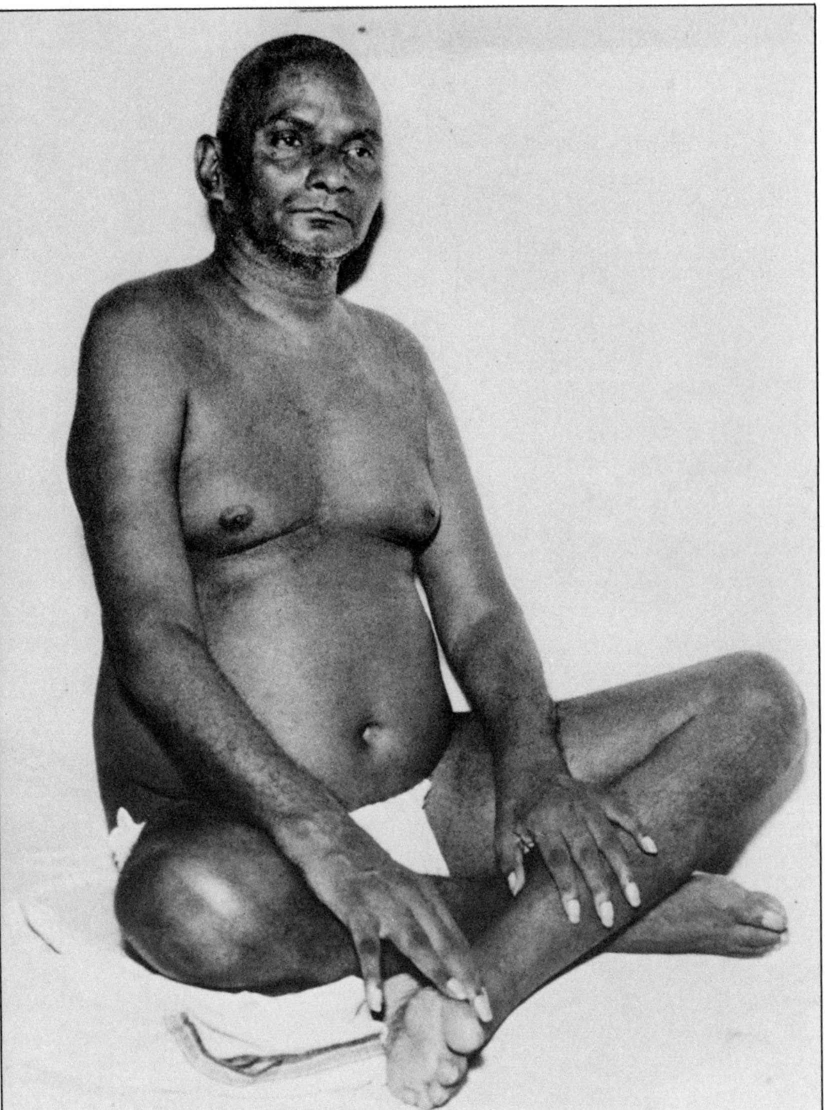

BHAGAVĀN NITYĀNANDA

Contents

SWĀMĪ MUKTĀNANDA

Introduction

Do not be lazy in *swādhyāya* (chanting and reciting sacred texts) — do not neglect it! *Swādhyāya* is, in fact, a way to study yourself. It has been practiced from time immemorial by great beings — enlightened beings, leaders, teachers, preceptors and fully realized masters — and they have inspired others to practice it as well. Revered Bāpūjī (Mahātmā Gandhi) never failed to hold his prayer or *swādhyāya* regularly. The seers say that it should be held every day with the unfailing regularity of the sun and moon, at an appointed hour, with deep feeling and reverence.

Swādhyāya increases inner radiance, mental vigor and agility. Its practice is far more uplifting than indulging in futile thoughts and unnecessary mental activity or following worthless tendencies. *Swādhyāya* embraces all aspects of yoga and grants all its rewards. Everyone sits in a clean place, in the lotus, perfect or easy posture, free from care, without moving or looking around. The book is held in the right hand, with the left hand on the left knee in the lion pose; both eyes are focused on the mantra text; and the ears are attuned to the neighboring voices — as well as one's own — chanting the divine names. Such practice of *swādhyāya* includes mastery of a posture *(āsana)*, a pose *(mudrā),* gazing at a fixed point *(trātaka)* and one-pointedness of mind *(dhyāna)* as one has to concentrate on the verses. This is concentration of a high order, since all mental energy is collected and directed toward mantras — reciting, hearing and seeing them. One then enjoys the flow of love released by mantras. Those who know only a few *āsanas,* a few *kriyās,* a few modes of ordinary *prāṇāyāma* and who think they are perfect despite their obvious imperfections can never appreciate the importance of the great yoga of *swādhyāya,* which is complete, perfect and fully rewarding in itself.

The divine name is the pure nectar of bliss. As one continues to chant, the mind becomes saturated with the mantras and easily achieves one-pointedness. The heart is stabilized on its goal and begins to taste the joy which is the inner essence of the mantras. It overcomes dreariness, and anxieties vanish. The smoldering coals of failure are extinguished and one becomes naturally absorbed in inner love and contentment. One realizes that the heart is the abode of deep peace, where love gushes, steadfastness is entrenched and the image of God shines forth. This is the glory of *swādhyāya.* The supreme and everlasting happiness that man longs for lies in inner purity alone. *Swādhyāya* is a subtle tonic that nourishes the inner being, imparts spiritual strength and purifies the mind and heart. Just as a man adorns his physical body with clothes and ornaments, and exercises to maintain health, similarly, he should take care of his inner spiritual body, developing its virtuous inclinations and beauty.

While describing the potency of the divine name, Haridas says: *japato hari-nāmāni sthāne śata-guṇādhikaḥ, ātmānaṁ ca punātyuccair japañ śrotṝn punāti ca* — "The name of God can be repeated in all times, places, circumstances and by all people. It may be beneficial to repeat other mantras silently, but the special power of the divine name lies in its being chanted loudly." The louder the chant, the greater its effect. He who repeats the name silently or in a low voice purifies himself alone, while he who sings it aloud also cleanses all those who hear it, including the inanimate as well as the animate. Toward the beginning of the morning chanting programs in our ashrams, we always chant the following lines:

Namo'stvanantāya sahasra-mūrtaye
sahasra-pādā'kṣi-śiroru-bāhave,
Sahasra-nāmne puruṣāya śāśvate
sahasra-koṭī-yuga-dhāriṇe namaḥ.

"Salutations to the infinite Lord, who has infinite forms, infinite feet, eyes, heads, thighs and arms. Salutations to the eternal being of infinite names, who supports millions of cosmic ages."

These lines praise the all-pervasive, formless, unmanifest absolute being who manifests Himself in a thousand forms. This is, in fact, true spiritual knowledge, the essence of science. Even physical science is making advances owing to its curiosity to know the boundless nature of the infinite, which embodies itself in innumerable shapes. Yet science is attempting to explore only a small portion of the vast cosmos which extends from the earth to Shiva and contains innumerable souls and innumerable worlds. Knowledge of the supreme is wisdom and also science, including all its various branches. The earth, the sky and outer space are the feet of that Lord whom man is trying to perceive with the eye of higher intelligence.

The next verse is:

Om namaḥ śivāya gurave
sac-cid-ānanda-mūrtaye,
Niṣprapañcāya śāntāya
nirālambāya tejase.

Who is invoked by the words *Om Namah Shivāya?* Who is remembered? Who can be met and spoken with through *Om Namah Shivāya?* Who is the one to address and praise, about whom numberless poems have been written and numberless hymns composed, from the dawn of creation to the present day? What is the nature of the supreme truth called Shiva, whose glories are sung by the serpent Shesha with his thousand tongues, his thousand uplifted heads? Who is continually praised by Saraswatī, holding the *vīnā* on her breast?

He to whom we kneel by uttering *Om Namah Shivāya* is the Guru, the Self of all, the embodiment of *sacchidānanda* — existence, consciousness and bliss absolute. *Sat* is the one who equally pervades all objects. The Self permeates all forms and is the ground of all. Whatever is perceived is based upon the *sat* aspect of God. No object can exist without a support. Just as gold forms the basis of different ornaments, and cotton of different garments, likewise God is the foundation of this entire universe. This Self, Shiva, the Guru, is responsible for the creation, sustenance and dissolution of the universe.

The second aspect of God is consciousness, *chit,* which illuminates all objects at all times and all places. That consciousness is also the pure light underlying the light of the sun, the moon, fire and all other lights of the universe.

God is also bliss, *ānanda,* which projects, maintains and finally withdraws the universe. If we reflect deeply, we will find that all the activities in the world reflect bliss; they are all motivated by bliss or the search for happiness. Why does man seek happiness in everything? Because God, the inner Self, is of the nature of bliss. Thus, in the Lord Sacchidānanda, we worship the being whose nature is existence-consciousness-bliss. Dwelling in everything as its inmost essence, the basis of love, supremely blissful, free from occupations and agitations *(niṣprapañcāya śāntāya),* He needs no other support *(nirālambāya)* and yet He sustains and supports all. He is the supreme effulgence *(tejase)* inhabiting the eyes and giving them light, residing in the tongue, the ears, the nose and other organs, perceiving all sense objects. He is God illuminating the entire universe from within and without.

It is Shrī Gurudeva, Nityānanda, who takes the individual soul to its source, which is pure consciousness, the Self, the origin of the universe. By his grace, all veils of impurities are torn asunder, restoring the mind in which Chiti Shakti has limited Herself to its boundlessness.

Nowhere but in the Guru will the disciple find one to uplift and transform him. Therefore, the Guru is worthy of the highest glory. As a *sādhaka* receives the sounds of these mantras from all sides, he enters a celestial realm.

After these mantras comes the main text, *Shrī Guru Gītā* or *Vishnu Sahasranāma*. The *Vishnu Sahasranāma* is a most significant, universal and uplifting japa yoga. It is pure ambrosia, a sublime scripture which gives the peace of salvation. It is a song of praise to the Lord dwelling in the heart. It dispels illnesses and gives robust health, increases knowledge, strength and fame and leads one to the realization of the Self of all.

If anyone were to ask me which is the one indispensable text, I would answer, "The *Guru Gītā*." This is so supremely holy that it makes the ignorant learned, the destitute wealthy and the scholarly fully realized. The *Guru Gītā* is a supreme song of Shiva, of salvation. It is a veritable ocean of bliss in this world. It encompasses the science of the absolute, the yoga of the Self. It gives vitality to life. It is a harmonious composition; its 182 stanzas in varied verse patterns beautifully describe the importance of devotion to the Guru, his role, his nature and his distinguishing characteristics. If a person who is devoted to the Guru sings this song, he easily attains all powers, realizations and knowledge, fulfilling the aim of yoga.

When Pārvatī, the ever-young Umā, or Kundalinī, the beloved consort of the great god Shiva, the ultimate goal of yogīs, whose nature is existence, consciousness and bliss, asked Her dearest Lord about the secret of the *Guru Gītā*, He replied that it bestows worldly fulfillment as well as spiritual liberation.

The truth is that only those pure and noble beings who are themselves fully immersed in devotion to the Guru and who worship him by identifying themselves with him are competent to write on the theme of the *Guru Gītā*. The mystery of the *Guru Gītā* can be comprehended only by such a saint as Jñāneshwar, who made a bull recite Vedic mantras, who moved a stone wall by the power and glory of his devotion to the Guru and who continually sang his praises though he himself was a teacher of teachers. Only such a being as Eknāth Mahārāj, the crest-jewel of all devotees of the Guru, who never tired of singing the Guru's praises, and whose devotion to the Guru pleased Lord Hari so much that He drew water for him, can adequately bring out the splendor of the *Guru Gītā*.

If someone were to ask me what gives meaning to my life, I would only say, "The name of my Guru." I discovered everything within me by my Guru's grace. Bhagavān Shrī Nityānanda was a perfect Guru. His essential teaching was: "The heart is the hub of all sacred places. Go there and roam in it." By remembering and worshipping such a master with the recitation of the *Guru Gītā,* one becomes holy. The Guru is indeed the god of gods. A great poet-saint, Mādhava Muni, says in a song: "I am only aware of the Guru's feet. I am ignorant of the *yamas* and *niyamas,* the prescriptions and prohibitions of yoga. Nor do I know any other method. I know only the Guru's feet. Is it not foolish to prefer gold to the philosophers' stone? Similarly, what is the use of salvation if it means renunciation of the Guru's feet?" This remarkable statement is full of deep meaning.

The *Guru Gītā,* devotion to the Guru, is my sole refuge. I am constantly repeating *Guru Om, Guru Om* and the *Guru Gītā* is played and recited every day. The Guru is my supreme goal.

In our ashrams, the recitations of holy texts such as the *Guru Gītā* and the *Shiva Mahimnah Stotram* are followed by sessions of chanting divine names, which release the flow of divine love, purifying the heart and stilling the mind.

Among the chants that are sung in the ashram are *Om Namah Shivāya; Shrī Rām Jay Rām; Hare Rāma Hare Krishna; Om Guru Jaya Guru; Shrī Krishna Govinda Hare Murāre; Om Namo Bhagavate; Gopālā Gopālā Devakīnandana Gopālā; Vitthale Vitthale; Shivāya Namah Om; Hari Hari Bol; Govinda Jaya Jaya; Rāma Rāghava; Nārāyana Nārāyana; Om Bhagavān; Jyota se Jyota; Gurudeva Hamārā Pyārā;* and many others. Everyone participates in the chanting with great fervor and enthusiasm. The chants are accompanied by various musical instruments such as the *ektārā, tamburā, tabla,* harmonium, tambourines, *kartāls,* and cymbals.

The morning and evening *Āratī* to the Lord is a noble practice which is very popular in India. In this way, gods, kings and men all honor their dear ones, the indwelling Lord and the Guru, who is the very Self of all. The *Āratī* is a sublime expression of love and adoration, a highly beneficial act.

Thus, *swādhyāya* performed with a melodious voice confers knowledge and meditation and cleanses the heart. It is a lofty spiritual practice. The truth is that man is an embodiment of sublime love, equanimity and peace. The supreme being dwells within you in His fullness. He witnesses the feeling, faith and love with which you chant, and He listens from within. He examines the quality of your devotion, love and faith. Therefore, sit for *swādhyāya* in a disciplined manner, full of love for the Lord, feeling that He is sitting by your side. Let your attention be concentrated on the mantras and their goal, on the sound of the chant, on your own Self; do not permit it to wander away. When the mind begins to roam, it becomes distracted, but when it turns within and is absorbed in *swādhyāya,* it becomes refined and perceptive. Sing sweetly and in tune, for the Lord hears every word you utter with great love, and He responds quickly to your feelings. Do not think He is remote. You have become alienated from the all-pervasive being because you have always considered Him to be far away. He is exceedingly close to you — closer than your breath.

My dear ones! So long as the indwelling Lord is not pleased, no one else can be pleased. When He is pleased, everyone is automatically pleased. Man should remain constantly aware of his duties. He was certainly not born just for eating, drinking and enjoying other sensuous pleasures until death overcomes him. Therefore, just as you value your material wealth, your children, wife, house, clothes and ornaments, you should also value your spiritual wealth in the form of *swādhyāya.*

As your mind becomes permeated with *swādhyāya,* you will be able to sleep soundly, wake up joyfully and live your life with delight and laughter. You will no longer be afraid of death nor worried about rebirth. You will be able to handle the practical side of your life skillfully, complete your studies enthusiastically and take care of your family without finding it a worldly burden. You will realize that the world is a veritable paradise. Above all, you will receive divine grace and finally realize your own divinity.

Swādhyāya is penance, wealth, near and dear ones — one's own inner Self. The all-pervasive spirit abides within you; that is the goal of *swādhyāya.* As long as you do not have a direct personal experience of the Self, continue to have full faith in the veracity of the one who has experienced it, without doubting or questioning. One day, it will make itself felt within you of its own accord. Such is the power of *swādhyāya.*

May you love all that you have received in the form of *swādhyāya* from the ancient seers, who are our highest well-wishers, and may you realize your own Self through it! May you always delight in your own inner being! May *swādhyāya* yield to you a rich harvest!

This is my blessing to you.

Your own,

SWĀMĪ MUKTĀNANDA

Ganeshpurī 1972

Notes on the Transliteration

The transliteration of Sanskrit, Hindi, and Marathi in the mantras in this book is that used internationally by students of these languages. It is not an exact phonetic transcription but it can easily be used as such, since the script of these languages, the Devanāgarī script, corresponds very regularly to the sounds. For a detailed explanation of the diacritical marks and a guide to Sanskrit pronunciation, see Appendix.

VOWELS

Vowels are short or long. Long vowels are indicated by a line above. A long vowel should be held for twice as long as a short one; in other words, *ā* should be held for the length of time it would take to pronounce two *a*'s.

The first eight are pure vowels, as in French or Italian, and the next two are diphthongs. The English equivalents are therefore approximate only.

a as in b*u*t, c*u*p	*ā* as in c*a*lm, f*a*ther
i as in b*i*t, s*i*t	*ī* as in s*ee*n, m*ea*n
u as in p*u*t, f*oo*t	*ū* as in r*oo*m, m*oo*d
e as in French l*e*s	*o* as in French b*eau*

ai, a diphthong, as in h*a*y, m*ai*ze

au, a diphthong, as in b*oug*h, n*o*w

ṛ, a semi-vowel, pronounced like a rolled *r* with a short *u* sound following it

A tilde, ~, over a vowel indicates that it should be pronounced nasally

CONSONANTS

c as in su*ch*

t, *d*, and *n* are pronounced with the tip of the tongue against the top teeth as in French

ṭ, *ḍ*, and *ṇ* are pronounced with the tip of the tongue bent back to touch the roof of the mouth

ś as in *sh*ine, *sh*ower

ṣ is pronounced like *ś* except that the tip of the tongue is bent back to touch the roof of the mouth

ñ as in o*ni*on, Spanish se*ñ*or

jñ as *dnya* or *gnya*

When consonants are followed by *h*, they should be aspirated

ḥ at the end of a sentence indicates that the previous vowel is echoed

Introductory Mantras

Sadgurunāth Mahārāj kī Jay

Hail the true Guru.

[*Om namaḥ*] *pārvatī-pataye*
Hara hara hara mahādev

Om! Salutations to Pārvatī's spouse. Hara, Hara, Hara, Mahādev!

Muktānanda mahān
jaya sadguru bhagavān
Jaya sadguru bhagavān

O great Muktānanda, glory to you who are the true Guru and the great Lord.

[*Om namaḥ*] *pārvatī-pataye*
Hara hara hara mahādev

Om! Salutations to Pārvatī's spouse. Hara, Hara, Hara, Mahādev!

Om guru jaya guru
saccidānanda guru
Saccidānanda guru
muktānanda sadguru

Om! O Guru, glory to you who are the embodiment of being, consciousness, and bliss.

O Muktānanda, the embodiment of being, consciousness, and bliss, you are the true Guru.

[*Om namaḥ*] *pārvatī-pataye*
Hara hara hara mahādev

Om! Salutations to Pārvatī's spouse. Hara, Hara, Hara, Mahādev!

Namo'stvanantāya sahasra-mūrtaye
sahasra-pādā'kṣi-śiroru-bāhave
Sahasra-nāmne puruṣāya śāśvate
sahasra-koṭī-yuga-dhāriṇe namaḥ

Salutations to the infinite Lord, who has infinite forms, infinite feet, eyes, heads, thighs, and arms. Salutations to the eternal being of infinite names, who supports millions of cosmic ages.

Om namaḥ śivāya gurave
sac-cid-ānanda-mūrtaye
Niṣprapañcāya śāntāya
nirālambāya tejase

Om. Salutations to the Guru, who is Shiva! His form is being, consciousness, and bliss. He is transcendent, calm, free from all support, and luminous.

Muktānandāya gurave
śiṣya-saṁsāra-hāriṇe
Bhakta-kāryaika-dehāya
namaste cit-sad-ātmane

Salutations to Muktānanda, the Guru, who rescues his disciples from the cycle of birth and death, who has assumed a body to meet the needs of his devotees, and whose nature is consciousness and being.

Om saha nāvavatu
Saha nau bhunaktu
Saha vīryam karavavahai
Tejasvi nāvadhītam astu
Mā vidviṣāvahai

Om. May we, Guru and disciple, be protected together. May we enjoy the fruits of our actions together. May we achieve strength together. May our knowledge be full of light. May we never have enmity for one another.

Om śāntiḥ śāntiḥ śāntiḥ

Om. Peace! Peace! Peace!

ŚRĪ GURU PĀDUKĀ-PAÑCAKAM

Five Stanzas on the Sandals of Shrī Guru

1. *Oṁ namo gurubhyo gurupādukābhyo*
   Namaḥ parebhyaḥ parapādukābhyaḥ,
   Acārya-siddheśvara-pādukābhyo
   Namo namaḥ śrīgurupādukābhyaḥ.

Om. Salutations to the Guru and the Guru's sandals. Salutations to the supreme (Guru) and to his supreme sandals. (Salutations) to the sandals of the spiritual teacher and the lord of Siddhas. Salutations again and again to Shrī Guru's sandals.

2. *Aiṅkāra-hrīṅkāra-rahasya-yukta-*
   Śrīṅkāra-gūḍhārtha-mahāvibhūtyā,
   Oṁkāra-marma-pratipādinībhyāṁ
   Namo namaḥ śrīgurupādukābhyām.

Salutations again and again to Shrī Guru's sandals, which are endowed with the mystery of (the seed letters) *aim* and *hrīm* and with the great glory of the profound meaning of (the seed letter) *shrīm* and which expound the secret of Om.

3. *Hotrāgni-hautrāgni-haviṣya-hotṛ-*
Homādi-sarvākṛti-bhāsamānam,
Yadbrahma tadbodha-vitāriṇībhyāṁ
Namo namaḥ śrīgurupādukābhyām.

Salutations again and again to Shrī Guru's sandals, which impart the knowledge of Brahman, who appears in all forms, such as Hotrāgni and Hautrāgni (the sacred sacrificial fires), the offerings, the priest, and the (ritualistic) sacrifice (itself).

4. *Kāmādi-sarpavraja-gāruḍābhyaṁ*
Viveka-vairāgya-nidhi-pradābhyām,
Bodhapradābhyāṁ drutamokṣadābhyāṁ
Namo namaḥ śrīgurupādukābhyām.

Salutations again and again to Shrī Guru's sandals, which serve as the Gāruda (the mantra against poison) to the multitude of serpents of desire and so on, which bestow the treasure of discrimination and dispassion, which grant true knowledge, and which give immediate liberation.

5. *Ananta-saṁsāra-samudra-tāra-*
Naukāyitābhyāṁ sthirabhaktidābhyām,
Jāḍyābdhi-saṁśoṣaṇa-vāḍavābhyāṁ
Namo namaḥ śrīgurupādukābhyām.

Salutations again and again to Shrī Guru's sandals, which are a boat (with which) to cross the endless ocean of the world, which bestow steadfast devotion, and which are a raging fire to dry the ocean of (spiritual) insensitivity.

Om śāntiḥ śāntiḥ śāntiḥ.

Om. Peace! Peace! Peace!

ŚRĪ GURU GĪTĀ

Song of the Guru

Om asya śrīgurugītā-stotra-mantrasya
bhagavān sadāśiva ṛṣiḥ.

Om. Lord Sadāshiva is the seer of the mantras of this hymn, *Shrī Guru Gītā.*

Nānāvidhāni chandāṁsi
śrīguruparamātmā devatā.

Its verse patterns are diverse. The Guru, the supreme Self, is its deity.

Haṁ bījaṁ saḥ śaktiḥ kroṁ kīlakaṁ
śrīguru-prasāda-siddhyarthe jape viniyogaḥ.

Ham is its seed letter, *sah* its power, and *krom* its nail. The purpose of repeating it is to win the Guru's grace.

Atha dhyānam.

Haṁsābhyāṁ parivṛtta-patra-kamalair
divyair jagat-kāraṇair,
Viśvotkīrṇamanekadehanilayaiḥ
svacchandam ātmecchayā.

Taddyotaṁ padaśāmbhavaṁ tu caraṇaṁ
dīpāṅkura-grāhiṇaṁ,
Pratyakṣākṣara-vigrahaṁ gurupadaṁ
dhyāyed vibhuṁ śāśvatam.

Now, meditation.

(The Guru, who dwells in) the lotus surrounded by the divine petals *ham* and *sah,* which reside in all beings and are the cause of the world, manifested the world in his own way and of his own free will. Meditate on the Guru, who reveals That, who is the expression of the *shāmbhava* state (Shivahood), who illumines like the flame of a lamp, who is eternal and all-pervasive, and who is a visible form of all letters.

Mama catur-vidha-puruṣārtha-siddhyarthe
jape viniyogaḥ.

I repeat the *Guru Gītā* to realize the four goals of life (*dharma,* righteousness; *artha,* wealth; *kāma,* pleasure; *moksha,* liberation).

Sūta uvāca:

1. *Kailāsa-śikhare ramye*
bhakti-sandhāna-nāyakam,
Praṇamya pārvatī bhaktyā
śaṅkaraṁ paryapṛcchata.

Sūta said:

On the beautiful summit of Mount Kailāsa, Pārvatī, having bowed with reverence to Lord Shiva, who is the master of uniting one with devotion, asked:

Śrī devyuvāca:

2. *Om namo deva deveśa*
   parātpara jagadguro,
   Sadāśiva mahādeva
   gurudīkṣāṁ pradehi me.

The Goddess said:
Om. Salutations, O God, O lord of gods, O higher than the highest, O teacher of the universe, O benevolent one, O great God, initiate me into the knowledge of the Guru.

3. *Kena mārgeṇa bho svāmin*
   dehī brahmamayo bhavet,
   Tvaṁ kṛpāṁ kuru me svāmin
   namāmi caraṇau tava.

O Lord, by which path can an embodied soul become one with Brahman (absolute reality)? Have compassion on me, O Lord! I bow to your feet.

Īśvara uvāca:

4. *Mamarūpāsi devi tvaṁ*
   tvat-prītyarthaṁ vadāmyaham,
   Lokopakārakaḥ praśno
   na kenāpi kṛtaḥ purā.

The Lord said:
O Goddess, you are My very Self. Out of love for you, I will tell you this. No one has ever asked this question before, which is a boon to all mankind.

5. *Durlabhaṁ triṣu lokeṣu*
   tacchṛṇuṣva vadāmyaham,
   Guruṁ vinā brahma nānyat
   satyaṁ satyaṁ varānane.

(This knowledge) is difficult to obtain in the three worlds. Listen to it. I will reveal it to you. Brahman is nothing other than the Guru. O beautiful one, this is the truth. This is the truth.

6. *Veda-śāstra-purāṇāni*
   itihāsādikāni ca,
   Mantra-yantrādi-vidyāśca
   smṛtir-uccāṭanādikam.

The Vedas (ancient scriptures), the Shāstras (religious books), the Purānas (texts of ancient legends), historical accounts, and other (writings); the science of mantra, *yantra* (mystical diagrams), and so on; the Smritis (traditional code of laws), magic incantations, and so on;

7. *Śaiva-śāktāgamādīni*
   anyāni vividhāni ca,
   Apabhraṁśa karāṇīha
   jīvānāṁ bhrāntacetasām.

The Shaiva and Shākta treatises and other various texts bring about in this world the downfall of those whose minds are deluded.

8. *Yajño vrataṁ tapo dānaṁ*
   japastīrthaṁ tathaiva ca,
   Gurutattvam avijñāya
   mūḍhāste carate janāḥ.

Those people are fools who engage in sacrificial rites, vows, penance, *japa,* charity, and also pilgrimages without knowing the Guru principle.

9. *Gurur buddhyātmano nānyat*
satyaṁ satyaṁ na saṁśayaḥ,
Tallābhārthaṁ prayatnastu
kartavyo hi manīṣibhiḥ.

The Guru is not different from the conscious Self. Without doubt, this is the truth, this is the truth. Therefore, wise men should make an effort to seek him.

10. *Gūḍha-vidyā jaganmāyā*
dehe cājñāna-sambhavā,
Udayo yatprakāśena
guruśabdena kathyate.

Māyā — the creator of the world, the veiled knowledge born of ignorance — resides in the body. He by whose light (true knowledge) arises is known by the word "Guru."

11. *Sarva-pāpa-viśuddhātmā*
śrīguroḥ pādasevanāt,
Dehī brahma bhavedyasmāt
tvatkṛpārthaṁ vadāmi te.

Out of compassion for you, I shall tell you how the embodied soul becomes Brahman, having been purified of all sins by serving the feet of Shrī Guru.

12. *Gurupādāmbujaṁ smṛtvā*
jalaṁ śirasi dhārayet,
Sarva-tīrthāvagāhasya
samprāpnoti phalaṁ naraḥ.

Sprinkle water on your head while remembering the lotus feet of the Guru. Thus, a person obtains the benefits of bathing in all holy waters.

13. *Śoṣaṇaṁ pāpa-paṅkasya*
dīpanaṁ jñāna-tejasām,
Gurupādodakaṁ samyak
saṁsārārṇava-tārakam.

The water of the Guru's feet (has the power) to dry up the mire of one's sins, to ignite the light of knowledge, and to take one smoothly across the ocean of this world.

14. *Ajñāna-mūla-haraṇaṁ*
janma-karma-nivāraṇam,
Jñāna-vairāgya-siddhyarthaṁ
gurupādodakaṁ pibet.

To obtain knowledge and detachment, sip the water of the Guru's feet, which destroys ignorance and ends karmas, (the cause of) rebirth.

15. *Guroḥ pādodakaṁ pītvā*
guror-ucchiṣṭabhojanam,
Gurumūrteḥ sadā dhyānaṁ
gurumantraṁ sadā japet.

Take a sip of the water of the Guru's feet, and eat the food that has been left by the Guru. Constantly meditate on the Guru's form, and always repeat the Guru's mantra.

16. *Kāśī-kṣetraṁ tannivāso*
jāhnavī caraṇodakam,
Gurur viśveśvaraḥ sākṣāt
tārakaṁ brahma niścitam.

His dwelling is the sacred (city of) Kāshī. The water of his feet is the (holy river) Gangā. The Guru himself is Vishveshvara (the Shiva of Kāshī). He is certainly the liberating mantra.

17. *Guroḥ pādodakaṁ yattu*
gayā'sau so'kṣayo vaṭaḥ,
Tīrtha-rājaḥ prayāgaśca
gurumūrtyai namo namaḥ.

The water of the Guru's feet (is the holiest water). He is Gayā (a holy center), he is (the holy) banyan tree Akshaya, and he is the most sacred Prayāga (the confluence of three holy rivers). Salutations again and again to the Guru.

18. *Gurumūrtiṁ smarennityaṁ*
gurunāma sadā japet,
Gurorājñāṁ prakurvīta
guror-anyanna bhāvayet.

Always remember the Guru's form. Constantly repeat the divine name given by the Guru. (Always) follow the Guru's commands. Think of nothing other than the Guru.

19. *Guruvaktra-sthitaṁ brahma*
prāpyate tatprasādataḥ,
Guror-dhyānaṁ sadā kuryāt
kulastrī svapateryathā.

The supreme knowledge that lies on the Guru's tongue can be realized through his grace. Always meditate on the Guru, just as a virtuous wife (constantly) thinks of her husband.

20. *Svāśramaṁ ca svajātiṁ ca*
svakīrti-puṣṭi-vardhanam,
Etatsarvaṁ parityajya
guror-anyanna bhāvayet.

Abandoning (thoughts of) all these — your stage in life, your caste, your reputation, and increasing your well-being — think of nothing other than the Guru.

21. *Ananyāś-cintayanto māṁ*
sulabhaṁ paramaṁ padam,
Tasmāt sarva-prayatnena
guror-ārādhanaṁ kuru.

The supreme state is easily attained by those who think of nothing else but Me. Therefore, strive to the utmost to propitiate the Guru.

22. *Trailokye sphuṭa-vaktāro*
devādyasura-pannagāḥ,
Guruvaktra-sthitā vidyā
gurubhaktyā tu labhyate.

In the three worlds gods, demons, snake-demons, and others clearly proclaim that the knowledge lying on the tongue of the Guru is obtained only through devotion to the Guru.

23. *Gukāras tvandhakāraśca*
rukāras teja ucyate,
Ajñāna-grāsakaṁ brahma
gurureva na saṁśayaḥ.

The syllable *gu* is darkness, and the syllable *ru* is said to be light. There is no doubt that the Guru is indeed the supreme knowledge that swallows (the darkness of) ignorance.

24. *Gukāraḥ prathamo varṇo*
māyādi-guṇa-bhāsakaḥ,
Rukāro dvitīyo brahma
māyā-bhrānti-vināśanam.

The first syllable *gu* represents the principles such as *māyā*, and the second syllable *ru* the supreme knowledge that destroys the illusion of *māyā*.

25. *Evaṁ gurupadaṁ śreṣṭhaṁ*
devānāmapi durlabham,
Hāhā-hūhū-gaṇaiścaiva
gandharvaiśca prapūjyate.

Thus, the state of the Guru is the highest, difficult even for gods to attain. It is worshipped by the followers of Hāhā and Hūhū and (other) *gandharvas* (celestial musicians).

26. *Dhruvaṁ teṣāṁ ca sarveṣāṁ*
nāsti tattvaṁ guroḥ param,
Āsanaṁ śayanaṁ vastraṁ
bhūṣaṇaṁ vāhanādikam.

27. *Sādhakena pradātavyaṁ*
guru-santoṣa-kārakam,
Guror-ārādhanaṁ kāryaṁ
svajīvitvaṁ nivedayet.

Surely for all these beings, there is no truth higher than the Guru. A seeker should offer a seat, a bed, clothing, ornaments, a vehicle, and other things that will please the Guru. He should gratify the Guru; he should dedicate his life to him.

28. *Karmaṇā manasā vācā*
nityam ārādhayed gurum,
Dīrgha-daṇḍaṁ namaskṛtya
nirlajjo gurusannidhau.

Prostrate fully before the Guru without reserve, and continually serve the Guru with mind, speech, and action.

29. *Śarīram indriyaṁ prāṇān*
sadgurubhyo nivedayet,
Ātmadārādikaṁ sarvaṁ
sadgurubhyo nivedayet.

Dedicate to the Sadguru the body, senses, and *prāna.* Dedicate to the Sadguru one's own wife and everything else.

30. *Kṛmi-kīṭa-bhasma-viṣṭhā*
durgandhi-malamūtrakam,
Śleṣma-raktaṁ tvacā-māṁsaṁ
vañcayenna varānane.

O beautiful one, do not withhold (from the Guru this body, which is full of) germs, worms, waste matter, foul-smelling urine and feces, phlegm, blood, skin, and flesh and (which is finally reduced) to ashes.

31. *Saṁsāravṛkṣam ārūḍhāḥ*
patanto narakārṇave,
Yena caivoddhṛtāḥ sarve
tasmai śrīgurave namaḥ.

Salutations to Shrī Guru, who indeed saved all (the devoted ones) who climbed the tree of the mundane world and were falling into the ocean of hell.

32. *Gururbrahmā gururviṣṇur*
gururdevo maheśvaraḥ,
Gurureva parabrahma
tasmai śrīgurave namaḥ.

The Guru is Brahmā. The Guru is Vishnu. The Guru is Lord Shiva. The Guru is indeed Parabrahman. Salutations to Shrī Guru.

33. *Hetave jagatāmeva*
saṁsārārṇava-setave,
Prabhave sarva-vidyānāṁ
śambhave gurave namaḥ.

Salutations to the Guru, who is Shiva, who is the only cause of the universe, who is the bridge (by which to) cross the ocean of the world, and who is the master of all knowledge.

34. *Ajñānatimirāndhasya*
jñānāñjana-śalākayā,
Cakṣur unmīlitaṁ yena
tasmai śrīgurave namaḥ.

Salutations to Shrī Guru, who with the collyrium stick of knowledge opens the eyes of one who is blinded by the darkness of ignorance.

35. *Tvaṁ pitā tvaṁ ca me mātā*
tvaṁ bandhustvaṁ ca devatā,
Saṁsāra-pratibodhārthaṁ
tasmai śrīgurave namaḥ.

Salutations to Shrī Guru. In order to receive the true understanding of the world, (I consider you to be) my father, my mother, my brother, and my God.

36. *Yatsatyena jagatsatyaṁ*
yatprakāśena bhāti tat,
Yadānandena nandanti
tasmai śrīgurave namaḥ.

Salutations to Shrī Guru, by whose reality the world is real, by whose light it is illumined, and by whose joy people are joyous.

37. *Yasya sthityā satyamidaṁ*
yadbhāti bhānurūpataḥ,
Priyaṁ putrādi yatprītyā
tasmai śrīgurave namaḥ.

Salutations to Shrī Guru, by whose existence the world exists, who shines through the form of the sun, and by whose love sons and others are dear to us.

38. *Yena cetayate hīdaṁ*
cittaṁ cetayate na yam,
Jāgrat-svapna-suṣuptyādi
tasmai śrīgurave namaḥ.

Salutations to Shrī Guru, who illumines this (world) but whom the mind cannot illumine. (He also illumines) the waking, dreaming, and deep sleep states.

39. *Yasya jñānādidaṁ viśvaṁ*
na dṛśyaṁ bhinnabhedataḥ,
Sadekarūparūpāya
tasmai śrīgurave namaḥ.

Salutations to Shrī Guru, whose only form is Truth and by whose knowledge this world will no longer be perceived to be divided by differences.

40. *Yasyāmataṁ tasya mataṁ*
mataṁ yasya na veda saḥ,
Ananya-bhāva-bhāvāya
tasmai śrīgurave namaḥ.

One who (thinks he) knows not, knows; one who (thinks he) knows, knows not. Salutations to Shrī Guru, whose thinking has no other thoughts (but those of the Absolute).

41. *Yasya kāraṇarūpasya*
kārya-rūpeṇa bhāti yat,
Kārya-kāraṇa-rūpāya
tasmai śrīgurave namaḥ.

Salutations to Shrī Guru, who appears as the effect (the universe) of which he is the cause. He is the cause as well as the effect.

42. *Nānārūpam-idaṁ sarvaṁ*
na kenāpyasti bhinnatā,
Kārya-kāraṇatā caiva
tasmai śrīgurave namaḥ.

All this (the universe) appears in various forms, but there is no difference (in him) from anything. It is merely (an illusion of) cause and effect. Salutations to Shrī Guru (who reveals this truth).

43. *Yadaṅghri-kamala-dvandvaṁ*
dvandva-tāpa-nivārakam,
Tārakaṁ sarvadā'padbhyaḥ
śrīguruṁ praṇamāmyaham.

I salute Shrī Guru, whose two lotus feet remove the pain of duality and who always protects one from calamities.

44. *Śive kruddhe gurustrātā*
gurau kruddhe śivo na hi,
Tasmāt sarva-prayatnena
śrīguruṁ śaraṇaṁ vrajet.

If Shiva is angry, the Guru saves you, but if the Guru is angry, even Shiva cannot save you. Therefore, with every effort take refuge in Shrī Guru.

45. *Vande gurupadadvandvaṁ*
vāṅmanaścittagocaram,
Śvetaraktaprabhābhinnaṁ
śivaśaktyātmakam param.

I salute the Guru's two feet, which are within the reach of speech, thought, and contemplation and which have different lusters—white and red—representing Shiva and Shakti.

46. *Gukāraṁ ca guṇātītaṁ*
rukāraṁ rūpavarjitam,
Guṇātītasvarūpaṁ ca
yo dadyātsa guruḥ smṛtaḥ.

The syllable *gu* is that which transcends all attributes, and the syllable *ru* is that which is without form. The Guru is said to be the one who bestows the state that is beyond attributes (and form).

47. *A-trinetraḥ sarvasākṣī*
a-caturbāhur acyutaḥ,
A-caturvadano brahmā
śrīguruḥ kathitaḥ priye.

O dear one, it is said that Shrī Guru is (Shiva), the witness of all, but without three eyes; he is Vishnu without four arms; he is Brahmā without four faces.

48. *Ayaṁ mayāñjalirbaddho*
dayā-sāgara-vṛddhaye,
Yad-anugrahato jantuś
citra-saṁsāra-muktibhāk.

I fold my hands (in salutation) so that the ocean of (the Guru's) compassion may increase. By his grace a mortal being is liberated from the diversified world.

49. *Śrīguroḥ paramaṁ rūpaṁ*
vivekacakṣuṣo'mṛtam,
Manda-bhāgyā na paśyanti
andhāḥ sūryodayaṁ yathā.

The supreme form of Shrī Guru is nectar to one who has the eye of discrimination. Those who are unfortunate cannot perceive this, just as the blind cannot see the sunrise.

50. *Śrīnātha-caraṇa-dvandvaṁ*
yasyāṁ diśi virājate,
Tasyai diśe namaskuryād
bhaktyā pratidinaṁ priye.

O beloved, every day you should bow with devotion in whichever direction Shrī Guru's two feet rest.

51. *Tasyai diśe satatam añjalireṣa ārye*
prakṣipyate mukharito madhupair budhaiśca,
Jāgarti yatra bhagavān gurucakravartī
viśvodaya-pralayanāṭaka-nityasākṣī.

O noble one, the wise always offer a handful of flowers humming with bees in the direction where Bhagavān, the sovereign Guru, is awake (residing). He is the eternal witness of the drama of the rise and the dissolution of this universe.

52. *Śrīnāthādi-gurutrayaṁ gaṇapatiṁ*
pīṭhatrayaṁ bhairavaṁ,
Siddhaughaṁ baṭukatrayaṁ padayugaṁ
dūtīkramaṁ maṇḍalam;

Vīrān-dvyaṣṭa-catuṣka-ṣaṣṭi-navakaṁ
vīrāvalī-pañcakaṁ,
Śrīman-mālini-mantra-rājasahitaṁ
vande guror maṇḍalam.

I bow to the Guru's assemblage, which is composed of the three preceding Gurus (whose titles) begin with Shrīnātha, Ganapati, three seats (of Shakti), (eight) Bhairavas, the group of (nine traditional) Siddhas, three Batukas, two feet (representing Shiva and Shakti), the sequence of (ten) Dūtīs, (three) Mandalas, ten Vīras, sixty-four (established Siddhas), nine (Mudrās), the line of five Vīras (with special functions), together with the revered Mālini (the letters of the alphabet), and the Mantrarāja.

53. *Abhyastaiḥ sakalaiḥ sudīrghamanilair*
vyādhi-pradair duṣkaraiḥ,
Prāṇāyāma-śatair anekakaraṇair
duḥkhātmakair durjayaiḥ.

Yasminnabhyudite vinaśyati balī
vāyuḥ svayaṁ tatkṣaṇāt,
Prāptuṁ tat sahajaṁ svabhāvam aniśaṁ
sevadhvamekaṁ gurum.

(What is the use of) practicing for so long all those hundreds of windy *prānāyāmas,* which are difficult and bring diseases, and the many yogic exercises, which are painful and difficult to master. Constantly serve only one Guru to attain that spontaneous and natural state. When it arises, the powerful *prāna* immediately stills of its own accord.

54. *Svadeśikasyaiva śarīracintanaṁ*
bhavedanantasya śivasya cintanam,
Svadeśikasyaiva ca nāmakīrtanaṁ
bhavedanantasya śivasya kīrtanam.

To contemplate the form of one's own Guru is to contemplate infinite Shiva. To sing the glory of the Guru's name is to sing the glory of infinite Shiva.

55. *Yatpāda-reṇu-kaṇikā*
kāpi saṁsāra-vāridheḥ,
Setubandhāyate nāthaṁ
deśikaṁ tamupāsmahe.

I worship the Lord Guru, even a few particles of dust from whose feet form a bridge across the ocean of the world.

56. *Yasmād anugrahaṁ labdhvā*
mahadajñānamutṣrjet,
Tasmai śrīdeśikendrāya
namaścābhīṣṭasiddhaye.

Receiving his grace, one gives up great ignorance. Salutations to the highest Guru for the attainment of the object of desire.

57. *Pādābjaṁ sarva-saṁsāra-*
dāvānala-vināśakam,
Brahmarandhre sitāmbhoja-
madhyasthaṁ candramaṇḍale.

The (Guru's) lotus feet, which extinguish the raging fires of all mundane existence, are situated in the center of the white lotus in the region of the moon in Brahmarandhra (the hollow space of the head).

58. *Akathādi-trirekhābje*
sahasradala-maṇḍale,
Haṁsa-pārśva-trikoṇe ca
smaret tanmadhyagaṁ gurum.

In the round space of the thousand-petaled lotus, there is a triangular lotus, which is formed by the three lines beginning with *a, ka,* and *tha* and which has *ham* and *sah* on two sides. One should remember the Guru, who is seated in its center.

59. *Sakala-bhuvana-sṛṣṭiḥ*
kalpitāśeṣapuṣṭir,
Nikhila-nigama-dṛṣṭiḥ
sampadāṁ vyarthadṛṣṭiḥ;

Avaguṇa-parimārṣṭis
tat-padārthaika-dṛṣṭir,
Bhava-guṇa-parameṣṭir
mokṣa-mārgaika-dṛṣṭiḥ.

60. *Sakala-bhuvana-raṅga-*
sthāpanā-stambhayaṣṭiḥ;
Sakaruṇa-rasa-vṛṣṭis
tattva-mālāsamaṣṭiḥ.

Sakala-samaya-sṛṣṭiḥ
saccidānanda-dṛṣṭir,
Nivasatu mayi nityaṁ
śrīguror divyadṛṣṭiḥ.

May the divine glance of the Guru ever dwell upon me. It creates all the worlds. It brings all nourishment. It has the viewpoint of all holy scriptures. It regards wealth as useless. It removes faults. It remains focused on the Ultimate. It is the highest ruler of the three *gunas,* which constitute the world. Its only goal is (to lead others on) the path of liberation. It is the central pillar supporting the stage of all the worlds. It showers the nectar of compassion. It is the aggregate of all *tattvas* (principles of creation). It creates all time. It is Sacchidānanda.

61. *Agni-śuddha-samaṁ tāta*
jvālā-paricakādhiyā,
Mantrarājamimaṁ manye
'harniśaṁ pātu mṛtyutaḥ.

O dear one, (having been thoroughly tested) by the intellect, which shines like a flame, I consider this, the greatest of the mantras (the *Guru Gītā*), to have been purified in the same way (that gold is purified) in fire.

62. *Tadejati tannaijati*
taddūre tatsamīpake,
Tadantarasya sarvasya
tadu sarvasya bāhyataḥ.

It (the Guru principle) moves and moves not. It is far as well as near. It is inside everything as well as outside everything.

63. *Ajo'hamajaro'haṁ ca*
anādinidhanaḥ svayam,
Avikāraś cidānanda
aṇīyān mahato mahān.

(Thus, the Guru knows): "I am unborn; I am free from old age. My being is without beginning or end. I am unchangeable. I am consciousness and bliss, smaller (than the smallest), greater than the greatest.

64. *Apūrvāṇāṁ paraṁ nityaṁ*
svayaṁjyotir nirāmayam,
Virajaṁ paramākāśaṁ
dhruvam-ānandamavyayam.

"I am beyond all primeval things. I am everlasting, self-luminous, taintless, and completely pure. I am the supreme ether. I am immovable, blissful, and imperishable."

65. *Śrutiḥ pratyakṣam aitihyam*
anumānaś catuṣṭayam,
Yasya cātmatapo veda
deśikaṁ ca sadā smaret.

Discern the (Guru's) spiritual power (through) the four (sources of knowledge) — the Vedas, direct perception, sacred historical texts, and inference. Always remember the Guru.

66. *Mananaṁ yadbhavaṁ kāryaṁ*
tadvadāmi mahāmate,
Sādhutvaṁ ca mayā dṛṣṭvā
tvayi tiṣṭhati sāmpratam.

O one of great intelligence, seeing your piety, I shall now tell you how to contemplate him.

67. *Akhaṇḍa-maṇḍalākāraṁ*
vyāptaṁ yena carācaram,
Tatpadaṁ darśitaṁ yena
tasmai śrīgurave namaḥ.

Salutations to Shrī Guru, who has revealed that state which pervades the entire sphere of this universe, which is composed of animate and inanimate objects.

68. *Sarva-śruti-śiroratna-*
virājita-padāṁbujaḥ,
Vedāntāmbuja-sūryo yas
tasmai śrīgurave namaḥ.

Salutations to Shrī Guru. His lotus feet are adorned with the crest-jewels (*mahāvākyas* — the great Upanishadic statements) of all Vedas. He is the sun to the lotus of Vedānta (in the sense that his light causes spiritual truths to bloom).

69. *Yasya smaraṇa-mātreṇa*
jñānam utpadyate svayam,
Ya eva sarva-samprāptis
tasmai śrīgurave namaḥ.

Salutations to Shrī Guru, merely by remembering whom knowledge arises spontaneously. He is all attainments.

70. *Caitanyaṁ śāśvataṁ śāntaṁ*
vyomātītaṁ nirañjanam,
Nāda-bindu-kalātītaṁ
tasmai śrīgurave namaḥ.

Salutations to Shrī Guru. He is consciousness, which is eternal, peaceful, stainless, and transcends the sky. He is beyond *nāda* (primordial sound), *bindu* (point containing the universe), and *kalā* (manifestation of the world).

71. *Sthāvaraṁ jaṅgamaṁ caiva*
tathā caiva carācaram,
Vyāptaṁ yena jagat sarvaṁ
tasmai śrīgurave namaḥ.

Salutations to Shrī Guru, who pervades this entire world, consisting of the movable and immovable and also the animate and inanimate.

72. *Jñāna-śakti-samārūḍhas*
tattvamālā-vibhūṣitaḥ,
Bhukti-mukti-pradātā yas
tasmai śrīgurave namaḥ.

Salutations to Shrī Guru. He is firmly established in the power of knowledge and is adorned with the garland of *tattvas.* He grants worldly fulfillment as well as salvation.

73. *Aneka-janma-samprāpta-*
sarva-karma-vidāhine,
Svātmajñāna-prabhāveṇa
tasmai śrīgurave namaḥ.

Salutations to Shrī Guru, who by (imparting) the power of Self-knowledge burns up all the karmas acquired through countless lifetimes.

74. *Na guroradhikaṁ tattvaṁ*
na guroradhikaṁ tapaḥ,
Tattvaṁ jñānātparaṁ nāsti
tasmai śrīgurave namaḥ.

Salutations to Shrī Guru. There is no truth higher than the Guru, no austerity greater than (service to) the Guru, no truth greater than the knowledge (of him).

75. *Mannāthaḥ śrījagannātho*
madgurus trijagadguruḥ,
Mamātmā sarva-bhūtātmā
tasmai śrīgurave namaḥ.

Salutations to Shrī Guru. My Lord is the lord of the universe. My Guru is the Guru of the three worlds. My Self is the Self of all beings.

76. *Dhyāna-mūlaṁ guror mūrtiḥ*
pūjā-mūlaṁ guroḥ padam,
Mantra-mūlaṁ guror vākyaṁ
mokṣa-mūlaṁ guroḥ kṛpā.

The root of meditation is the Guru's form. The root of worship is the Guru's feet. The root of mantra is the Guru's word. The root of liberation is the Guru's grace.

77. *Gururādir anādiśca*
guruḥ parama-daivatam,
Guroḥ parataraṁ nāsti
tasmai śrīgurave namaḥ.

Salutations to Shrī Guru. The Guru is the beginning (of all, but) he is without a beginning. The Guru is the supreme deity. There is nothing higher than the Guru.

78. *Sapta-sāgara-paryanta-*
tīrtha-snānādikaṁ phalam,
Guror-aṅghri-payobindu-
sahasrāṁśe na durlabham.

The merit gained by bathing in all holy waters, up to the seven seas, is not difficult to obtain by (sipping even) one-thousandth part of a drop of the water from the Guru's feet.

79. *Harau ruṣṭe gurustrātā*
gurau ruṣṭe na kaścana,
Tasmāt sarva-prayatnena
śrīguruṁ śaraṇaṁ vrajet.

If Lord Hari (Vishnu) is angry, the Guru protects you, but if the Guru is angry, no one can save you. Therefore, make every effort to take refuge in Shrī Guru.

80. *Gurureva jagatsarvaṁ*
brahma-viṣṇu-śivātmakam,
Guroḥ paratarаṁ nāsti
tasmāt sampūjayed gurum.

Indeed, the Guru is the whole universe, consisting of Brahmā, Vishnu, and Shiva. There is nothing higher than the Guru. Therefore, worship the Guru.

81. *Jñānaṁ vijñāna-sahitaṁ*
labhyate gurubhaktitaḥ,
Guroḥ parataraṁ nāsti
dhyeyo'sau gurumārgibhiḥ.

By devotion to the Guru, one obtains knowledge as well as wisdom. There is nothing higher than the Guru. Followers of the Guru should meditate on him.

82. *Yasmāt parataraṁ nāsti*
neti netīti vai śrutiḥ,
Manasā vacasā caiva
nityam ārādhayed gurum.

Nothing exists which is higher than he. The Vedas describe him as "not this, not this." Therefore, always worship the Guru with mind and speech.

83. *Guroḥ kṛpā-prasādena*
brahma-viṣṇu-sadāśivāḥ,
Samarthāḥ prabhavādau ca
kevalaṁ gurusevayā.

It is by the grace of the Guru and only through service to the Guru that Brahmā, Vishnu, and Shiva become capable of creation (sustenance, and destruction).

84. *Deva-kinnara-gandharvāḥ*
pitaro yakṣa-cāraṇāḥ,
Munayo'pi na jānanti
guruśuśrūṣaṇe vidhim.

Gods, *kinnaras, gandharvas, pitris, yakshas, chāranas* (all beings of different orders), and even sages do not know the proper manner of serving the Guru.

85. *Mahāhaṅkāragarveṇa*
tapo-vidyā-balānvitāḥ,
Saṁsāra-kuharāvarte
ghaṭa-yantre yathā ghaṭāḥ.

Due to inflated ego and pride, (even) those equipped with the power of austerity and learning (continue to revolve) in the vortex of worldly life, like pots on a water wheel.

86. *Na muktā devagandharvāḥ*
pitaro yakṣakinnarāḥ,
Ṛṣayaḥ sarvasiddhāśca
gurusevā-parāṅmukhāḥ.

(Even) gods, *gandharvas, pitris, yakshas, kinnaras,* seers, and all Siddhas are not liberated if they are averse to serving the Guru.

87. *Dhyānaṁ śṛṇu mahādevi*
sarvānanda-pradāyakam,
Sarva-saukhyakaraṁ nityaṁ
bhukti-mukti-vidhāyakam.

O great Goddess, listen to the (method of) meditation (on the Guru), which grants all joys, always brings all happiness, and gives worldly fulfillment as well as liberation.

88. *Śrīmat-parabrahma guruṁ smarāmi*
śrīmat-parabrahma guruṁ vadāmi,
Śrīmat-parabrahma guruṁ namāmi
śrīmat-parabrahma guruṁ bhajāmi.

I remember Shrī Guru, who is Parabrahman. I speak of Shrī Guru, who is Parabrahman. I bow to Shrī Guru, who is Parabrahman. I worship Shrī Guru, who is Parabrahman.

89. *Brahmānandaṁ paramasukhadaṁ*
kevalaṁ jñānamūrtiṁ,
Dvandvātītaṁ gaganasadṛśaṁ
tattvamasyādilakṣyam;

Ekaṁ nityaṁ vimalam acalaṁ
sarvadhī-sākṣi-bhūtaṁ,
Bhāvā-tītaṁ triguṇa-rahitaṁ
sadguruṁ taṁ namāmi.

I bow to the Sadguru, who is the bliss of Brahman and the bestower of the highest joy. He is absolute. He is knowledge personified. He is beyond duality, (all-pervasive) like the sky, and the object of (the great Upanishadic statement) "Thou art That." He is one. He is eternal. He is pure. He is steady. He is the witness of all thoughts. He is beyond all modifications (of mind and body) and free from the three *gunas.*

90. *Nityaṁ śuddhaṁ nirābhāsaṁ*
nirākāraṁ nirañjanam,
Nityabodhaṁ cidānandaṁ
guruṁ brahma namāmyaham.

I bow to the Guru, who is Brahman, eternal and pure. He is beyond perception, formless, and without taint. He is eternal knowledge, consciousness, and bliss.

91. *Hṛdambuje karṇika-madhya-saṁsthe*
siṁhāsane saṁsthita-divyamūrtim,
Dhyāyed guruṁ candra-kalā-prakāśaṁ
cit-pustakābhīṣṭavaraṁ dadhānam.

Meditate on the divine form of the Guru seated on the throne situated in the center of the pericarp of the heart lotus, shining like the crescent of the moon, holding the book of knowledge and (the *mudrā* that) bestows the desired boon.

92. *Śvetāmbaraṁ śveta-vilepa-puṣpaṁ*
muktā-vibhūṣaṁ muditaṁ dvinetram,
Vāmāṅka-pīṭha-sthita-divyaśaktiṁ
mandasmitaṁ sāndra-kṛpā-nidhānam.

He has two eyes. He is clad in white garments. He is besmeared with white paste and is adorned with (garlands of) white flowers and pearls. He is joyous. He has a gentle smile. He is a treasure house of abundant grace. The divine Shakti is seated on the left side of his lap.

93. *Ānandamānandakaraṁ prasannaṁ*
jñānasvarūpaṁ nijabodhayuktam,
Yogīndramīḍyaṁ bhavarogavaidyaṁ
śrīmadguruṁ nityamahaṁ namāmi.

I always bow to Shrī Guru, who is bliss, who exudes delight, and who is cheerful. His very nature is knowledge, and he is aware of his own Self. He is highest among the yogīs and is adorable. He is the physician for the disease of worldly existence.

94. *Yasmin sṛṣṭisthitidhvaṁsa-*
nigrahānugrahātmakam,
Kṛtyaṁ pañcavidhaṁ śaśvad
bhāsate taṁ namāmyaham.

I bow to him (the Guru) in whom the five types of functions — creation, sustenance, dissolution, control, and the bestowal of grace — are constantly revealed.

95. *Prātaḥ śirasi śuklābje*
dvinetraṁ dvibhujaṁ gurum,
Varābhayayutaṁ śāntaṁ
smaret taṁ nāmapūrvakam.

In the morning, reciting the divine name, think of the two-eyed, two-armed, peaceful Guru (seated) in the white lotus in the head and endowed with (the *mudrās* of the hands) granting boons and fearlessness.

96. *Na guroradhikaṁ na guroradhikaṁ*
na guroradhikaṁ na guroradhikam,
Śivaśāsanataḥ śivaśāsanataḥ
śivaśāsanataḥ śivaśāsanataḥ.

There is nothing greater than the Guru. There is nothing greater than the Guru. There is nothing greater than the Guru. There is nothing greater than the Guru.

This is the teaching of Shiva. This is the teaching of Shiva. This is the teaching of Shiva. This is the teaching of Shiva.

97. *Idameva śivaṁ tvidameva śivaṁ*
tvidameva śivaṁ tvidameva śivam,
Mama śāsanato mama śāsanato
mama śāsanato mama śāsanataḥ.

This, indeed, is Shiva. Indeed, this too is Shiva. Indeed, this too is Shiva. Indeed, this too is Shiva.

This is my command. This is my command. This is my command. This is my command.

98. *Evaṁvidhaṁ guruṁ dhyātvā*
jñānam utpadyate svayam,
Tatsadguru-prasādena
mukto'hamiti bhāvayet.

Through meditation on the Guru in this manner, knowledge arises spontaneously. Therefore, one should feel, "I am liberated by the grace of the Sadguru."

99. *Gurudarśitamārgeṇa*
manaḥśuddhiṁ tu kārayet,
Anityaṁ khaṇḍayet sarvaṁ
yatkiñcid-ātmagocaram.

One should purify one's mind by following the path shown by the Guru. Whatever transient things are ascribed to the Self should be discarded.

100. *Jñeyaṁ sarvasvarūpaṁ ca*
jñānaṁ ca mana ucyate,
Jñānaṁ jñeyasamaṁ kuryān
nānyaḥ panthā dvitīyakaḥ.

The essential nature of everything is worthy of being known. It is said that the mind is knowledge (because knowledge is obtained through the mind). One should consider knowledge to be identical with the object of knowledge. There is no way other than that (to liberation).

101. *Evaṁ śrutvā mahādevi*
gurunindāṁ karoti yaḥ,
Sa yāti narakaṁ ghoraṁ
yāvac-candradivākarau.

O great Goddess, he who speaks ill of the Guru in spite of hearing all this falls into the most dreadful hell and (remains there) as long as the sun and moon shine.

102. *Yāvat kalpāntako dehas*
tāvadeva guruṁ smaret,
Gurulopo na kartavyaḥ
svacchando yadi vā bhavet.

Continue to remember the Guru as long as the body lasts, even to the end of the universe. One should never forsake the Guru, even if he behaves in a self-willed manner.

103. *Huṅkāreṇa na vaktavyaṁ*
prājñaiḥ śiṣyaiḥ kathañcana,
Guroragre na vaktavyam
asatyaṁ ca kadācana.

Wise disciples should never speak egotistically and should never tell a lie before the Guru.

104. *Guruṁ tvaṁkṛtya huṁkṛtya*
guruṁ nirjitya vādataḥ,
Araṇye nirjale deśe
sa bhaved brahmarākṣasaḥ.

One who speaks to the Guru in rude or insulting terms or who wins arguments with him is born as a demon in a jungle or in a waterless region.

105. *Munibhiḥ pannagairvāpi*
surairvā śāpito yadi,
Kālamṛtyubhayādvāpi
gurū rakṣati pārvati.

O Pārvatī, the Guru protects one if one is cursed by sages, snake-demons, or even gods and also (frees one) from the fear of time and death.

106. *Aśaktā hi surādyāśca*
aśaktā munayas tathā,
Guruśāpena te śīghraṁ
kṣayaṁ yānti na saṁśayaḥ.

Surely, gods and others are powerless, as also the sages are powerless; being cursed by the Guru, they soon perish. There is no doubt of it.

107. *Mantrarājam idaṁ devi*
gururityakṣaradvayam,
Smṛtivedārthavākyena
guruḥ sākṣāt paraṁ padam.

O Goddess, this word "Guru," composed of two letters (*gu* and *ru*), is the greatest of mantras. According to the words of the Vedas and Smritis, the Guru is the highest reality itself.

108. *Śrutismṛtī avijñāya*
kevalaṁ gurusevakāḥ,
Te vai sannyāsinaḥ proktā
itare veṣadhāriṇaḥ.

Indeed, only the Guru's (devoted) servants are called true *sannyāsīs,* even though they may not know the Vedas and Smritis. All others are merely wearing the clothes (of a *sannyāsī*).

109. *Nityaṁ brahma nirākāraṁ*
nirguṇaṁ bodhayet param,
Sarvaṁ brahma nirābhāsaṁ
dīpo dīpāntaraṁ yathā.

Just as one lamp lights another lamp, (the Guru) imparts the knowledge that everything is Brahman — the Brahman that is imperceptible, eternal, highest, without form, and without attributes.

110. *Guroḥ kṛpāprasādena*
ātmārāmaṁ nirīkṣayet,
Anena gurumārgeṇa
svātmajñānaṁ pravartate.

One should perceive the inner Self through the gift of the Guru's grace. By this path of the Guru, knowledge of one's Self arises.

111. *Ābrahmastambaparyantaṁ*
paramātmasvarūpakam,
Sthāvaraṁ jaṅgamaṁ caiva
praṇamāmi jaganmayam.

I bow to (the Guru, who is) the highest being and who is of the form of this world, from Brahmā to a blade of grass, (everything) movable and immovable.

112. *Vande'haṁ saccidānandaṁ*
bhedātītaṁ sadā gurum,
Nityaṁ pūrṇaṁ nirākāraṁ
nirguṇaṁ svātmasaṁsthitam.

I always bow to the Guru, who is Sacchidānanda, who transcends all differences, who is eternal, perfect, without form, and without attributes, and who is established in his own Self.

113. *Parāt paratararaṁ dhyeyaṁ*
nityam-ānandakārakam,
Hṛdayākāśa-madhyasthaṁ
śuddha-sphaṭika-sannibham.

The Guru, who is higher than the highest, who always bestows bliss, and who is seated in the center of the space of the heart, (shining) like a pure crystal, should be meditated upon.

114. *Sphaṭika-pratimā-rūpaṁ*
dṛśyate darpaṇe yathā,
Tathātmani cidākāraṁ
ānandaṁ so'hamityuta.

Just as the image of a crystal is seen in a mirror, so the bliss, which is consciousness, (is reflected) in the Self and (the realization comes), "Indeed, I am That."

115. *Aṅguṣṭha-mātra-puruṣaṁ*
dhyāyataś cinmayaṁ hṛdi,
Tatra sphurati bhāvo yaḥ
śṛṇu taṁ kathayāmyaham.

Listen, I shall speak to you of the feeling that arises when one meditates on the thumb-sized being in the heart, who is consciousness.

116. *Agocaraṁ tathā'gamyaṁ*
nāma-rūpa-vivarjitam,
Niḥśabdaṁ tadvijānīyāt
svabhāvaṁ brahma pārvati.

O Pārvatī, know that the nature of Brahman is beyond perception, beyond understanding, without name and form, and without sound (and other attributes perceptible by the senses).

117. *Yathā gandhaḥ svabhāvena*
karpūra-kusumādiṣu,
Śītoṣṇādi-svabhāvena
tathā brahma ca śāśvatam.

As fragrance is natural in flowers, camphor, and other things and as cold and heat are natural (in water and fire), so is Brahman eternal.

118. *Svayaṁ tathāvidho bhūtvā*
sthātavyaṁ yatrakutracit,
Kīṭabhramaravat tatra
dhyānaṁ bhavati tādṛśam.

After becoming (aware that one is) like That (Brahman), one may live anywhere. (Then) wherever one is, one's meditation (on the Guru) becomes like that of the worm on the wasp.

119. *Gurudhyānaṁ tathā kṛtvā*
svayaṁ brahmamayo bhavet,
Piṇḍe pade tathā rūpe
mukto'sau nātra saṁśayaḥ.

By meditating on the Guru, one becomes Brahman. There is no doubt that one is liberated in *pinda, pada,* and *rūpa.*

Śrī pārvatyuvāca:

120. *Piṇḍaṁ kiṁ tu mahādeva*
padaṁ kiṁ samudāhṛtam,
Rūpātītaṁ ca rūpaṁ kiṁ
etadākhyāhi śaṅkara.

Shrī Pārvatī said:
O great God, what is *pinda?* What is known as *pada?* What are *rūpa* and *rūpātīta?* O Shankara, explain this to me.

Śrī mahādeva uvāca:

121. *Piṇḍaṁ kuṇḍalinī-śaktiḥ*
padaṁ haṁsamudāhṛtam,
Rūpaṁ binduriti jñeyaṁ
rūpātītaṁ nirañjanam.

Shrī Mahādeva said:
Pinda is Kundalinī Shakti. *Hamsa* (spontaneous repetition of Hamsa) is *pada.* Know *rūpa* to be the *bindu* (blue pearl), and *rūpātīta* is the pure One (beyond the three).

122. *Piṇḍe muktā pade muktā*
rūpe muktā varānane,
Rūpātīte tu ye muktās
te muktā nātra saṁśayaḥ.

O beautiful one, they are liberated in *pinda* (whose Kundalinī is awake). They are liberated in *pada* (who hear spontaneous repetition of Hamsa). They are liberated in *rūpa* (who have envisioned the blue pearl). But they are undoubtedly liberated who are liberated in *rūpātīta* (who experience the transcendental state beyond form).

123. *Svayaṁ sarvamayo bhūtvā*
paraṁ tattvaṁ vilokayet,
Parāt-parataraṁ nānyat
sarvam etan nirālayam.

Becoming one with everything, a person should perceive the highest truth. There is nothing higher than the highest. All this is without (any particular) abode (because it is all-pervasive).

124. *Tasyāvalokanaṁ prāpya*
sarva-saṅga-vivarjitaḥ,
Ekākī niḥspṛhaḥ śāntas
tiṣṭhāset tatprasādataḥ.

Having perceived It by his (the Guru's) grace, remain solitary, tranquil, without desires, and without any attachment.

125. *Labdhaṁ vā'tha na labdhaṁ vā*
svalpaṁ vā bahulaṁ tathā,
Niṣkāmenaiva bhoktavyaṁ
sadā santuṣṭa-cetasā.

Whether you attain it or you do not attain it, whether it is great or small, it should always be enjoyed without desire and with a contented mind.

126. *Sarvajñapadam-ityāhur*
dehī sarvamayo budhāḥ,
Sadānandaḥ sadā śānto
ramate yatrakutracit.

The wise say that the all-knowing state is that in which the embodied soul becomes one with everything. (Then), being ever-blissful and ever-tranquil, he rejoices wherever he may be.

127. *Yatraiva tiṣṭhate so'pi*
sa deśaḥ puṇya-bhājanam,
Muktasya lakṣaṇaṁ devi
tavāgre kathitaṁ mayā.

Wherever he lives, that place becomes an abode of merit. O Goddess, I have described to you the characteristics of a liberated one.

128. *Upadeśas tathā devi*
gurumārgeṇa muktidaḥ,
Guru-bhaktis tathā dhyānaṁ
sakalaṁ tava kīrtitam.

O Goddess, also (I have given you) the teaching according to the path of the Guru which brings liberation. I have also fully explained to you devotion to the Guru and meditation (on him).

129. *Anena yad bhavet kāryaṁ*
tad vadāmi mahāmate,
Lokopakārakaṁ devi
laukikaṁ tu na bhāvayet.

O one of great intelligence, I shall now tell you the things that are accomplished by this (recitation of the *Guru Gītā*). O Goddess, (the powers accruing from this) should not be used for selfish gains, but for the welfare of people.

130. *Laukikāt karmaṇo yānti*
jñānahīnā bhavārṇavam,
Jñānī tu bhāvayet sarvaṁ
karma niṣkarma yat-kṛtam.

The ignorant ones who work for selfish ends sink into the ocean of worldly existence, whereas a knower of Truth considers all the actions he does to be non-action.

131. *Idaṁ tu bhaktibhāvena*
paṭhate śṛṇute yadi,
Likhitvā tat-pradātavyaṁ
tat-sarvaṁ saphalaṁ bhavet.

If one reads and hears this (the *Guru Gītā*) with devotion, one should make a copy to give to others. This will all bear fruit.

132. *Gurugītātmakaṁ devi*
śuddha-tattvaṁ mayoditam,
Bhava-vyādhi-vināśārthaṁ
svayameva japet sadā.

O Goddess, I have told you the pure truth in the form of the *Guru Gītā*. One should always repeat it to oneself to overcome the disease of wordly existence.

133. *Gurugītākṣaraikaṁ tu*
mantrarājam imaṁ japet,
Anye ca vividhā mantrāḥ
kalāṁ nārhanti ṣoḍaśīm.

Even one letter of the *Guru Gītā* is a supreme mantra. One should repeat it. All other mantras of diverse kinds are not worth even one-sixteenth part of it.

134. *Anantaphalam āpnoti*
gurugītā-japena tu,
Sarva-pāpa-praśamanaṁ
sarva-dāridrya-nāśanam.

Surely, by repeating the *Guru Gītā* one obtains endless rewards. It destroys all sins and ends all privations.

135. *Kālamṛtyubhayaharaṁ*
sarvasaṅkaṭanāśanam,
Yakṣarākṣasabhūtānāṁ
coravyāghrabhayāpaham.

It delivers one from the fear of time and death. It puts an end to all misfortunes. It removes the fear of spirits, demons, ghosts, thieves, and tigers.

136. *Mahā-vyādhi-haraṁ sarvaṁ*
vibhūti-siddhidaṁ bhavet,
Athavā mohanaṁ vaśyaṁ
svayameva japet sadā.

It eradicates all major diseases. It confers prosperity and superhuman powers or the ability to captivate and control others. One should always repeat it to oneself.

137. *Vastrāsane ca dāridryaṁ*
pāṣāṇe rogasambhavaḥ,
Medinyāṁ duḥkhamāpnoti
kāṣṭhe bhavati niṣphalam.

(Repeating the *Guru Gītā*) on a seat of cloth brings poverty, on stone it brings disease, on the earth it brings unhappiness, and on wood it becomes fruitless.

138. *Kṛṣṇājine jñānasiddhir*
mokṣaśrīr vyāghracarmaṇi,
Kuśāsane jñānasiddhiḥ
sarvasiddhistu kambale.

The skin of a black deer brings the attainment of (indirect) knowledge. A tiger skin begets the splendor of liberation. A seat of *kusha* grass brings the attainment of (direct) knowledge. A woolen blanket brings all attainments.

139. *Kuśairvā dūrvayā devi*
āsane śubhrakambale,
Upaviśya tato devi
japed ekāgramānasaḥ.

O Goddess, (the *Guru Gītā*) should be repeated (by one) with a one-pointed mind (who is) sitting on a seat of *kusha* or *dūrva* grass covered with a white blanket.

140. *Dhyeyaṁ śuklaṁ ca śāntyarthaṁ*
vaśye raktāsanaṁ priye,
Abhicāre kṛṣṇavarṇaṁ
pītavarṇaṁ dhanāgame.

O beloved, one should think of a white seat for peace, a red one for the power to control (others), a black one to exorcise evil spirits, and a yellow one to acquire wealth.

141. *Uttare śāntikāmastu*
vaśye pūrvamukho japet,
Dakṣiṇe māraṇaṁ proktaṁ
paścime ca dhanāgamaḥ.

One should repeat (the *Guru Gītā*) facing north if one desires peace, facing east for the power to control (others); it is said that one should face south to destroy (evil spirits) and face west to acquire wealth.

142. *Mohanaṁ sarvabhūtānāṁ*
bandhamokṣakaraṁ bhavet,
Deva-rāja-priyakaraṁ
sarva-loka-vaśaṁ bhavet.

It (the repetition of the *Guru Gītā*) attracts all beings and brings release from bondage. It gains the affection of Indra (the lord of heaven) and brings control over all the worlds.

143. *Sarveṣāṁ stambhanakaraṁ*
guṇānāṁ ca vivardhanam,
Duṣkarma-nāśanaṁ caiva
sukarma-siddhidaṁ bhavet.

It grants the power to paralyze all (hostile creatures), it nurtures good qualities, it stops (the fruition of) bad actions, and it also brings about the fruition of good deeds.

144. *Asiddhaṁ sādhayet kāryaṁ*
navagraha-bhayāpaham,
Duḥsvapna-nāśanaṁ caiva
susvapna-phala-dāyakam.

It accomplishes unfinished tasks, delivers one from fear of (harm from the) nine planets, puts an end to bad dreams, and makes good dreams come true.

145. *Sarvaśāntikaraṁ nityaṁ*
tathā vandhyāsuputradam,
Avaidhavyakaraṁ strīṇāṁ
saubhāgyadāyakaṁ sadā.

It always bestows peace in all respects, grants a good son to a barren woman, averts women's widowhood, and always brings good fortune.

146. *Āyurārogyamaiśvarya-*
putrapautrapravardhanam,
Akāmataḥ strī vidhavā
japān mokṣamavāpnuyāt.

It increases longevity, health, affluence, (and grants) children and grandchildren. If a widow repeats it without desire, she obtains salvation.

147. *Avaidhavyaṁ sakāmā tu*
labhate cānyajanmani,
Sarvaduḥkhabhayaṁ vighnaṁ
nāśayecchāpahārakam.

(If she repeats it) with desire, she will not become a widow in her next lifetime. It removes all miseries, fears, and obstacles, and delivers one from curses.

148. *Sarva-bādhā-praśamanaṁ*
dharmārtha-kāma-mokṣa-dam,
Yaṁ yaṁ cintayate kāmaṁ
taṁ taṁ prāpnoti niścitam.

It removes all hurdles and grants (the four goals of life): righteousness, wealth, pleasure, and liberation. One definitely obtains whatever desire one may entertain.

149. *Kāmitasya kāmadhenuḥ*
kalpanā-kalpa-pādapaḥ,
Cintāmaṇiś cintitasya
sarva-maṅgala-kārakam.

(The *Guru Gītā*) is the wish-fulfilling cow for one who has desires. It is the wish-fulfilling tree that makes fantasies come true. It is the wish-fulfilling gem for one's thoughts. It brings good luck in every way.

150. *Mokṣahetur japennityaṁ*
mokṣaśriyam avāpnuyāt,
Bhoga-kāmo japedyo vai
tasya kāma-phala-pradam.

One whose goal is liberation should repeat it regularly. He attains the splendor of liberation. One who repeats it with the desire for enjoyment will, indeed, get the fruit of his wish.

151. *Japecchāktaśca sauraśca*
gāṇapatyaśca vaiṣṇavaḥ,
Śaivaśca siddhidaṁ devi
satyaṁ satyaṁ na saṁśayaḥ.

A follower of Shakti, the Sun, Ganapati, Vishnu, or Shiva should repeat (the *Guru Gītā*). O Goddess, it will accomplish (his objective). Without doubt, this is the truth. This is the truth.

152. *Atha kāmyajape sthānaṁ*
kathayāmi varānane,
Sāgare vā sarittīre
'thavā hariharālaye.

O beautiful one, now I shall describe the places to repeat it for the fulfillment of desires: on the seashore, on a river bank, or in a temple of Vishnu or Shiva;

153. *Śakti-devālaye goṣṭhe*
sarva-devālaye śubhe,
Vaṭe ca dhātrīmūle vā
maṭhe vṛndāvane tathā.

In a shrine of Shakti, in a cowshed, in all holy temples of gods, in an ashram, under a banyan tree or a *dhātrī* tree, or in a thicket of *tulsi* plants.

154. *Pavitre nirmale sthāne*
nityānuṣṭhānato'pi vā,
Nirvedanena maunena
japametaṁ samācaret.

One should repeat it in silence and with detachment in a clean and pure place, whether one recites it daily or for a certain number of times.

155. *Śmaśāne bhayabhūmau tu*
vaṭamūlāntike tathā,
Sidhyanti dhauttare mūle
cūtavṛkṣasya sannidhau.

(All actions) are accomplished by repeating it in a cremation ground, in frightful places, near the root of a banyan tree, under a thorn-apple tree, or near a mango tree.

156. *Guruputro varaṁ mūrkhas*
tasya sidhyanti nānyathā,
Śubhakarmāṇi sarvāṇi
dīkṣā-vrata-tapāṁsi ca.

Even a fool who is a son (a devoted disciple) of the Guru is better (than one who is learned but not a devoted disciple). All his actions such as initiation, vows, and penance bear fruit. It cannot be otherwise.

157. *Saṁsāra-mala-nāśārthaṁ*
bhava-pāśa-nivṛttaye,
Gurugītāmbhasi snānaṁ
tattvajñaḥ kurute sadā.

One who knows the Truth always bathes in the waters of the *Guru Gītā* to wash away his worldly impurities and to become free from the snares of worldly existence.

158. *Sa eva ca guruḥ sākṣāt*
sadā sadbrahmavittamaḥ,
Tasya sthānāni sarvāṇi
pavitrāṇi na saṁśayaḥ.

He (the devoted disciple) himself becomes the Guru. (Then) he is always the foremost among the knowers of Brahman. There is no doubt that for him all places are holy.

159. *Sarva-śuddhaḥ pavitro'sau*
svabhāvādyatra tiṣṭhati,
Tatra devagaṇāḥ sarve
kṣetre pīṭhe vasanti hi.

He is holy and pure in all respects. Whatever region or dwelling he happens to live in becomes inhabited by the multitude of gods.

160. *Āsanasthaḥ śayāno vā*
gacchaṁstiṣṭhan-vadannapi,
Aśvārūḍho gajārūḍhaḥ
supto vā jāgṛto'pi vā.

Whether he is asleep or awake, sitting or lying down, standing or moving around or speaking, riding a horse, or sitting on an elephant;

161. *Śuciṣmāṁśca sadā jñānī*
gurugītā-japena tu,
Tasya darśana-mātreṇa
punarjanma na vidyate.

In fact, through the recitation of the *Guru Gītā,* a knower of the Truth is always pure. By merely having his darshan one is not born again.

162. *Samudre ca yathā toyaṁ*
kṣīre kṣīraṁ ghṛte ghṛtam,
Bhinne kumbhe yathākāśas
tathātmā paramātmani.

Just as water (merges) in the ocean, milk in milk, *ghee* in *ghee,* the space (inside the pot in the space outside) when a pot is broken, so the individual soul (merges) in the universal soul.

163. *Tathaiva jñānī jīvātmā*
paramātmani līyate,
Aikyena ramate jñānī
yatra tatra divāniśam.

In the very same way, the realized soul is merged in the highest Self. Day and night, wherever he may be, the realized being delights in his identity (with the supreme being).

164. *Evaṁvidho mahāmuktaḥ*
sarvadā vartate budhaḥ,
Tasya sarva-prayatnena
bhāva-bhaktiṁ karoti yaḥ.

165. *Sarva-sandeha-rahito*
mukto bhavati pārvati,
Bhukti-mukti-dvayaṁ tasya
jihvāgre ca sarasvatī.

A wise person, fully liberated, always lives in this manner. O Pārvatī, one who serves him wholeheartedly and with deep devotion is relieved of all doubts and is liberated. Both worldly enjoyments and liberation come to him. Saraswatī (the goddess of speech and learning) (dwells) on the tip of his tongue.

166. *Anena prāṇinaḥ sarve*
gurugītā-japena tu,
Sarva-siddhiṁ prāpnuvanti
bhuktiṁ muktiṁ na saṁśayaḥ.

There is no doubt that by this repetition of the *Guru Gītā* all beings do, indeed, obtain all powers, pleasures, and liberation.

167. *Satyaṁ satyaṁ punaḥ satyaṁ*
dharmyaṁ sāṅkhyaṁ mayoditam,
Gurugītāsamaṁ nāsti
satyaṁ satyaṁ varānane.

It is the truth. It is the truth. It is always the truth that the knowledge revealed by Me is worthy of being followed. There is nothing like the *Guru Gītā.* O beautiful one, this is the truth. This is the truth.

168. *Eko deva ekadharma*
eka-niṣṭhā paraṁ tapaḥ,
Guroḥ parataraṁ nānyan
nāsti tattvaṁ guroḥ param.

(To follow) one God, one religion, and one faith is the highest austerity. There is nothing higher than the Guru. No truth is greater than the Guru.

169. *Mātā dhanyā pitā dhanyo*
dhanyo vaṁśaḥ kulaṁ tathā,
Dhanyā ca vasudhā devi
gurubhaktiḥ sudurlabhā.

Blessed is the mother (of a devoted disciple), blessed is the father, blessed is the family and ancestry. Blessed is the earth (on which he walks). O Goddess, (such) devotion to the Guru is very rare.

170. *Śarīram indriyaṁ prāṇāś*
cārthaḥ svajanabāndhavāḥ,
Mātā pitā kulaṁ devi
gurureva na saṁśayaḥ.

There is no doubt, O Goddess, that only the Guru is the body, the senses, the vital breath, the wealth, and (both) close and distant relatives. He is the father, the mother, the (entire) family.

171. *Ākalpa-janmanā koṭyā*
japavrata-tapaḥ-kriyāḥ,
Tat-sarvaṁ saphalaṁ devi
guru-santoṣa-mātrataḥ.

O Goddess, actions such as mantra repetition, vows, and the austerities (practiced) through millions of births since the beginning of the universe — all those bear fruit only when the Guru is pleased.

172. *Vidyā-tapo-balenaiva*
manda-bhāgyāśca ye narāḥ,
Gurusevāṁ na kurvanti
satyaṁ satyaṁ varānane.

Those people who do not serve the Guru are unfortunate, even with the power of their learning and austerities. O beautiful one, this is the truth. This is the truth.

173. *Brahma-viṣṇu-maheśāśca*
devarṣi-pitṛ-kinnarāḥ,
Siddha-cāraṇa-yakṣāśca
anye'pi munayo janāḥ.

Brahmā, Vishnu, Shiva, divine seers, *pitris, kinnaras,* Siddhas, *chāranas, yakshas,* sages, and other people (attained their respective powers only through devotion to the Guru).

174. *Guru-bhāvaḥ paraṁ tīrtham*
anyatīrthaṁ nirarthakam,
Sarva-tīrthāśrayaṁ devi
pādāṅguṣṭhaṁ ca vartate.

Gurubhāva (absorption in the Guru) is the most sacred place; every other place of pilgrimage is meaningless. O Goddess, the big toe of the Guru's (right) foot is the abode of all places of pilgrimage.

175. *Japena jayamāpnoti*
cānantaphalam āpnuyāt,
Hīnakarma tyajan sarvaṁ
sthānāni cādhamāni ca.

By abandoning all mean actions and degraded places and reciting (the *Guru Gītā*), one obtains success and endless rewards.

176. *Japaṁ hīnāsanaṁ kurvan*
hīnakarma-phala-pradam,
Gurugītāṁ prayāṇe vā
saṅgrāme ripusaṅkaṭe.

177. *Japañ jayamavāpnoti*
maraṇe muktidāyakam,
Sarva-karma ca sarvatra
guruputrasya sidhyati.

Repetition (of the *Guru Gītā*) on an improper *āsana* bears (the same) fruit as mean actions. While on a journey, on a battlefield, or in the face of a dangerous enemy, one obtains success by repeating the *Guru Gītā.* At the time of death it brings liberation. All the actions of the Guru's son (a devoted disciple) are accomplished everywhere.

178. *Idaṁ rahasyaṁ no vācyaṁ*
tavāgre kathitaṁ mayā,
Sugopyaṁ ca prayatnena
mama tvaṁ ca priyā tviti.

Do not disclose this secret that I have revealed to you. It should be well guarded with every effort. (I have revealed it to you) because you are so dear to me.

179. *Svāmi-mukhya-gaṇeśādi-*
viṣṇvādīnāṁ ca pārvati,
Manasāpi na vaktavyaṁ
satyaṁ satyaṁ vadāmyaham.

Do not impart this even mentally to Ganesha and among others of whom Swāmi (Kārttikeya, son of Pārvatī) is the chief, nor to Vishnu or other (gods). I speak the truth, the only truth.

180. *Atīva-pakvacittāya*
śraddhā-bhakti-yutāya ca,
Pravaktavyamidaṁ devi
mamātmā'si sadā priye.

O Goddess, explain it only to one whose mind is fully matured and who is endowed with faith and devotion. O beloved, you are My very Self forever.

181. *Abhakte vañcake dhūrte*
pākhaṇḍe nāstike nare,
Manasāpi na vaktavyā
gurugītā kadācana.

Never impart the *Guru Gītā* even mentally to a person who is without devotion, a cheat, a rogue, a hypocrite, or a heretic.

182. *Saṁsāra-sāgara-samuddharaṇaika-mantraṁ*
brahmādi-devamuni-pūjita-siddha-mantram,
Dāridrya-duḥkha-bhavaroga-vināśa-mantraṁ
vande mahābhaya-haraṁ gururāja-mantram.

I bow to the Gururāja mantra (the *Guru Gītā*), which removes the great fear (of transmigration). It is the only mantra that rescues one from the ocean of the world. It is the perfected mantra worshipped by sages and gods, such as Brahmā and others. It is the mantra that puts an end to privations, miseries, and the disease of mundane existence.

Iti śrīskandapurāṇe
uttarakhaṇḍe īśvarapārvatīsaṁvāde
gurugītā samāptā.
Śrī gurudeva-caraṇārpaṇamastu.

Thus ends the *Guru Gītā,* which occurs in the dialogue between Shiva and Pārvatī in the latter portion of *Shrī Skanda Purāna.*

This is offered at the feet of Shrī Gurudeva.

ŚRĪ AVADHŪTA STOTRAM

Hymn Praising the Avadhūt

1. *Nityānandāya gurave*
   śiṣya-saṁsāra-hāriṇe,
   Bhakta-kāryaika-dehāya
   namaste cit-sad-ātmane.

Salutations to Nityānanda, the Guru, who rescues his disciples from transmigration, who has assumed a body for the needs of devotees, whose nature is consciousness and being.

2. *Nirvāsanaṁ nirākāṅkṣaṁ*
   sarva-doṣa-vivarjitam,
   Nirālambaṁ nirātaṅkaṁ
   nityānandaṁ namāmyaham.

Free of desires, free of expectations, free of all defects, independent and fearless—to that Nityānanda, I bow.

3. *Nirmamaṁ nirahaṅkāraṁ*
   sama-loṣṭāśma-kāñcanam,
   Sama-duḥkha-sukhaṁ dhīraṁ
   hyavadhūtaṁ namāmyaham.

Free of possessiveness, free of egoism, regarding as the same a clod, a stone, and gold, even-minded in happiness and sorrow, all-enduring—to that *avadhūt,* indeed, I bow.

4. *Avināśinaṁ ātmānaṁ*
hyekaṁ vijñāya tattvataḥ,
Vīta-rāga-bhaya-krodhaṁ
nityānandaṁ namāmyaham.

"Indestructible is the Self, for it is one." Having known this truth, he is free of attachment, fear, and anger—to that Nityānanda, I bow.

5. *Nāhaṁ deho na me deho*
jīvo nāham ahaṁ hi cit,
Evaṁ vijñāya santuṣṭaṁ
hyavadhūtaṁ namāmyaham.

"I am not the body, nor is the body mine; I am not a bound soul, for I am consciousness." Thus reflecting, he is content—to that *avadhūt,* indeed, I bow.

6. *Samastaṁ kalpanā-mātraṁ*
hyātmā muktaḥ sanātanaḥ,
Iti vijñāya santṛptaṁ
nityānandaṁ namāmyaham.

"The entire universe is only a mental construct; the Self alone is free and eternal." Thus reflecting, he is satisfied—to that Nityānanda, I bow.

7. *Jñānāgni-dagdha-karmāṇaṁ*
kāma-saṅkalpa-varjitam,
Heyopādeya-hīnaṁ taṁ
hyavadhūtaṁ namāmyaham.

His deeds burned up by the fire of realization, purged of desire and ambition, free of the need to accept or reject—to that *avadhūt,* indeed, I bow.

8. *Svabhāvenaiva yo yogī*
sukhaṁ bhogaṁ na vāñchati,
Yadṛcchā-lābha-santuṣṭaṁ
nityānandaṁ namāmyaham.

Possessing the innate disposition of a yogī, he does not long for pleasure and enjoyment; he is content with whatever comes unsought — to that Nityānanda, I bow.

9. *Naiva nindā-praśaṁsābhyāṁ*
yasya vikrīyate manaḥ,
Ātma-krīḍaṁ mahātmānaṁ
hyavadhūtaṁ namāmyaham.

Not even by blame or praise is his mind perturbed; sporting in the Self, great-souled — to that *avadhūt,* indeed, I bow.

10. *Nityaṁ jāgrad-avasthāyāṁ*
svapna-vadyo'vatiṣṭhate,
Niścintaṁ cinmayātmānaṁ
nityānandaṁ namāmyaham.

Always in the waking state, he abides like one asleep; free of anxiety, his mind the nature of pure consciousness — to that Nityānanda, I bow.

11. *Dveṣyaṁ nāsti priyaṁ nāsti*
nāsti yasya śubhāśubham,
Bheda-jñāna-vihīnaṁ taṁ
hyavadhūtaṁ namāmyaham.

To him none is hateful, none is dear; for him there is no good or bad. Free of the knowledge of difference — to that *avadhūt,* indeed, I bow.

12. *Jaḍaṁ paśyati no yastu*
jagat paśyati cinmayam,
Nitya-yuktaṁ guṇātītaṁ
nityānandaṁ namāmyaham.

To him nothing is insentient; the whole world is filled with consciousness. Joined with the eternal, having passed beyond the *gunas* — to that Nityānanda, I bow.

13. *Yo hi darśana-mātreṇa*
pavate bhuvana-trayam,
Pāvanaṁ jaṅgamaṁ tīrthaṁ
hyavadhūtaṁ namāmyaham.

He indeed, by a mere glance, purifies the three worlds; he is the movable, the immovable, and all holy places — to that *avadhūt*, indeed, I bow.

14. *Sarva-pūjyaṁ sadā pūrṇaṁ*
hyakhaṇḍānanda-vigraham,
Sva-prakāśaṁ cid-ānandaṁ
nityānandaṁ namāmyaham.

An object of worship for all, forever perfect, an embodiment of bliss, indivisible, shining by his own light, reveling in blissful consciousness — to that Nityānanda, I bow.

15. *Niṣkalaṁ niṣkriyaṁ śāntaṁ*
nirmalaṁ paramāmṛtam,
Gaṇeśapurī-vāsinaṁ
hyavadhūtaṁ namāmyaham.

Undivided, performing no actions, calm, spotless, supremely nectarean, dwelling at Ganeshpurī — to that *avadhūt,* indeed, I bow.

16. *Yoga-pūrṇaṁ tapo-mūrtiṁ*
prema-pūrṇaṁ sudarśanam,
Jñāna-pūrṇaṁ kṛpā-mūrtiṁ
nityānandaṁ namāmyaham.

Perfect in yoga, an embodiment of austerity, full of love, being of auspicious countenance, perfect in realization, an embodiment of grace—to that Nityānanda, I bow.

Universal Prayer

1. *Durjanaḥ sajjano bhūyāt*
   sajjanaḥ śāntim āpnuyāt,
   Śānto mucyeta bandhebhyo
   muktaś cānyān vimocayet.

May the wicked become good. May the good obtain peace. May the peaceful be freed from bonds. May the freed set others free.

2. *Svasti prajābhyaḥ paripālayantāṁ*
   nyāyyena mārgeṇa mahīṁ mahīśāḥ,
   Go-brāhmaṇebhyaḥ śubham astu nityaṁ
   lokāḥ samastāḥ sukhino bhavantu.

Blessings on the subjects of those who are ruling, and may these great lords rule the earth in a just manner. May good always be the lot of cows and Brāhmins. May all people be happy.

3. *Kāle varṣatu parjanyaḥ*
   pṛthivī śasya-śālinī,
   Deśo'yaṁ kṣobha-rahito
   brāhmaṇāḥ santu nirbhayāḥ.

May it rain at the right time. May the earth have storehouses full of grain. May this country be free of disturbances. May Brāhmins be free of persecution.

4. *Sarve bhavantu sukhinaḥ*
sarve santu nirāmayāḥ,
Sarve bhadrāṇi paśyantu
mā kaścid-duḥkha-bhāg-bhavet.

May all be happy. May all be healthy. May all see only auspicious sights. May no one have a share in sorrow.

5. *Sarvas taratu durgāṇi*
sarvo bhadrāṇi paśyatu,
Sarvaḥ kāmān avāpnotu
sarvaḥ sarvatra nandatu.

May everyone surmount his difficulties. May everyone see only auspicious sights. May everyone have his desires fulfilled. May everyone everywhere be glad.

6. *Svasti mātra uta pitre no astu*
svasti gobhyo jagate puruṣebhyaḥ,
Viśvaṁ subhūtaṁ suvidatraṁ no astu
jyogeva dṛśyema sūryam.

May blessings fall on our mother and father; blessings on the cows, the fields, the workers. May everything of ours flourish and be an aid to knowledge. And long may we see the sun.

Om śāntiḥ śāntiḥ śāntiḥ.
Om. Peace! Peace! Peace!

JYOTA SE JYOTA

Prayer

Jyota se jyota jagāvo
Sadguru jyota se jyota jagāvo

Refrain:
Merā antara timira miṭāvo
Sadguru jyota se jyota jagāvo

Light my lamp from your lamp, O Sadguru; light my lamp from your lamp. Remove the darkness covering my heart.

1. *He yogeśvara he jñāneśvara (2x)*
He sarveśvara he parameśvara (2x)
Nija kṛpā barasāvo
Sadguru jyota se jyota jagāvo
(Refrain)

O lord of yoga, O lord of knowledge, O lord of all, O supreme master, shower your grace upon us.

2. *Hama bālaka tere dvāra pe āye (2x)*
Maṅgala darasa dikhāvo
Sadguru jyota se jyota jagāvo
(Refrain)

We, your children, have come to your door. Show us your auspicious form.

3. *Śīśa jhukāya karẽ terī āratī (2x)*
Prema sudhā barasāvo
Sadguru jyota se jyota jagāvo
(Refrain)

We worship you, bowing our heads low. Shower the nectar of your love upon us.

4. *Antara mẽ yuga yuga se soī (2x)*
Citi śakti ko jagāvo
Sadguru jyota se jyota jagāvo
(Refrain)

It has been sleeping within us for ages. Awaken that Chiti Shakti.

5. *Sācī jyota jage hṛdaya mẽ (2x)*
So'ham nāda jagāvo
Sadguru jyota se jyota jagāvo
(Refrain)

The true flame is alive in our hearts. Awaken us to the So'ham music.

6. *Jīvana muktānanda avināśī (2x)*
Caraṇana śaraṇa lagāvo
Sadguru jyota se jyota jagāvo
(Refrain)

O imperishable Muktānanda! Let our lives be dedicated to your feet.

7. *Tvameva mātā ca pitā tvameva*
Tvameva bandhuśca sakhā tvameva
Tvameva vidyā draviṇaṁ tvameva
Tvameva sarvaṁ mama deva deva

You are the mother, you are the father, you are the brother, you are the friend. You are knowledge, you are wealth. You are everything for me, O god of gods.

8. *Dūra karo duḥkha darda saba*
Dayā karo bhagavān
Mana mandir mẽ ujjvala ho
Terā nirmala jñān

Remove all my cares and sorrows. Be merciful, O Lord! May the temple of my mind be illumined by your pure knowledge!

9. *Jisa ghara mẽ ho āratī*
Caraṇa-kamala cita lāy
Tahā̃ hari vāsā kare
Jyota ananta jagāy

In every home where lights are waved to you and where your lotus feet are adored, there dwells Lord Hari in His infinite glory.

10. *Jahā̃ bhakta kīrtana kare*
Bahe prema dariyā
Tahā̃ hari śravaṇa kare
Satya loka se āy

Wherever devotees sing your names and praises, and streams of love flow, there Lord Hari descends from His own true realm to listen.

11. *Saba kucha diyā āpa ne*
Bhẽṭa karũ kyā nāth
Namaskāra kī bhẽṭa karũ
Joḍũ maĩ donõ hāth (2x)

You have given me everything. What shall I offer to you, O master? With folded hands, I offer salutations.

Om pūrṇamadaḥ pūrṇamidaṁ
Pūrṇāt pūrṇamudacyate
Pūrṇasya pūrṇamādāya
Pūrṇamevāvaśiṣyate

Om. That is perfect. This is perfect. From the perfect springs the perfect. If the perfect is taken from the perfect, the perfect remains.

Om śāntiḥ śāntiḥ śāntiḥ

Om. Peace! Peace! Peace!

Sadgurunāth Mahārāj kī Jay
Hail the true Guru.

SADGURU KĪ ĀRATĪ

Wave Lights to the True Guru

Refrain:
Āratī karū̃ sadguru kī karū̃
sadguru kī pyāre guruvara kī
Āratī karū̃ guruvara kī (2x)

Let me perform *āratī* for the true Guru. Let me perform for the true Guru, for the beloved best of Gurus. Let me perform *āratī* for the best of Gurus.

1. *Jaya gurudeva amala avināśī*
jñānarūpa antara ke vāsī (2x)
Paga-paga para dete prakāśa
jaise kiraṇẽ dinakara kī
Āratī karū̃ guruvara kī
(Refrain)

Hail, divine Guru, pure, indestructible, dwelling within us in the form of knowledge, illuminating every step like the rays of the sun. Let me perform *āratī* for the best of Gurus.

2. *Jaba se śaraṇa tumhārī āye*
amṛta se mīṭhe phala pāye (2x)
Śaraṇa tumhārī kyā hai chāyā
kalpavṛkṣa taruvara kī
Āratī karū̃ guruvara kī
(Refrain)

When we first came to your refuge, we obtained the sweet fruit of eternal life. Your shelter is like the shade of the wish-fulfilling tree in heaven that grants all one's desires. Let me perform *āratī* for the best of Gurus.

3. *Brahmajñāna ke pūrṇa prakāśaka*
yogajñāna ke aṭala pravartaka (2x)
Jaya guru-caraṇa-saroja miṭā dī
vyathā hamāre ura kī
Āratī karū̃ guruvara kī
(Refrain)

He fully reveals the knowledge of the Godhead; he is an expert exponent of the knowledge of yoga. Hail the dust of the Guru's lotus feet, which has removed the pain from our hearts. Let me perform *āratī* for the best of Gurus.

4. *Andhakāra se hamẽ nikālā*
dikhalāyā hai amara ujāla (2x)
Kaba se jāne chāna rahe the
khāka suno dara-dara kī
Āratī karū̃ guruvara kī
(Refrain)

He has led us out of darkness; he has shown us the immortal flame. Listen, for so long we were (fools) going around from door to door just picking up dust. Let me perform *āratī* for the best of Gurus.

5. *Sā̃śaya miṭā viveka karāyā*
bhavasāgara se pāra lā̃ghāyā (2x)
Amara pradīpa jalākara kara dī
niśā dūra isa tana kī
Āratī karū̃ guruvara kī
(Refrain)

He has made us develop discrimination. He has removed our doubts and brought us across the sea of birth and death. Having lit the lamp of eternal life, he has removed the night from our bodies. Let me perform *āratī* for the best of Gurus.

6. *Bhedõ bīca abheda batāyā*
   āvāgamana vimukta karāyā (2x)
   Dhanya hue hama pākara dhārā
   brahmajñāna nirjhara kī
   Āratī karū̃ guruvara kī
   (Refrain)

He has revealed the undifferentiated in the midst of differences. He has delivered us from transmigration. We are fortunate to have obtained the clear stream of knowledge of the Godhead. Let me perform *āratī* for the best of Gurus.

7. *Karo kṛpā sadguru jaga-tārana*
   satpatha-darśaka bhrānti-nivārana (2x)
   Jaya ho nitya jyoti dikhalāne
   vāle līlādhara kī
   Āratī karū̃ guruvara kī
   (Refrain)

Give us your grace, true Guru, to help us cross over the world. Show us the true path; dispel wrong ideas. Hail the one who has revealed the eternal light and whose existence is a divine play. Let me perform *āratī* for the best of Gurus.

8. *Muktānanda he sadguru dātā*
   śaktipāta ke divya pradātā (2x)
   Kara ke vāsa gaṇeśapurī
   bhava-bādhā hara lī jana kī
   Āratī karū̃ guruvara kī
   (Refrain)

O Muktānanda, you are the true Guru, the giver, the divine bestower of *shaktipāt*. Having taken up your abode at Ganeshpurī, you have delivered people from the obstacle of (the cycle of) birth and death. Let me perform *āratī* for the best of Gurus.

Om caitanyaṁ śāśvataṁ śāntaṁ
vyomātītaṁ nirañjanam
Nāda-bindu-kalātītaṁ
tasmai śrīgurave namaḥ

Om. The Guru is consciousness, eternal, peaceful, beyond space, stainless. He is beyond *nāda-bindu-kalā*. I bow to that Guru.

Sadgurunāth Mahārāj kī Jay
Hail the true Guru.

Śrī Kṛṣṇa Govinda Hare Murāre
He Nātha Nārāyaṇa Vāsudeva

VIṢṆU SAHASRANĀMA

Introduction to the Thousand Names of Vishnu

1. *Yasya smaraṇa-mātreṇa*
   janma-saṁsāra-bandhanāt,
   Vimucyate namas tasmai
   viṣṇave prabhaviṣṇave.

By the mere remembrance of Him, one is freed from the bondage of birth and transmigration. I bow to that Vishnu, the creator of the universe.

2. *Namaḥ samasta-bhūtānām*
   ādibhūtāya bhū-bhṛte,
   Aneka-rūpa-rūpāya
   viṣṇave prabhaviṣṇave.

I bow to the first manifested of all manifestations, who upholds the earth, who has the form of the manifold, Vishnu, the creator.

Vaiśampāyana uvāca:

3. *Śrutvā dharmān aśeṣeṇa*
   pāvanāni ca sarvaśaḥ,
   Yudhiṣṭhiraḥ śāntanavaṁ
   punarevābhyabhāṣata.

Vaishampāyana said:
Having heard about all the purifying duties *(dharmas)* exhaustively, Yudhishthira said to the son of Shantanu (Bhīshma):

Yudhiṣṭhira uvāca:

4. *Kim-ekaṁ daivataṁ loke*
kiṁ-vāpy-ekaṁ parāyaṇam,
Stuvantaḥ kaṁ kam-arcantaḥ
prāpnuyur mānavāḥ śubham.

Yudhishthira said:
What is the sole divinity in the world? In other words, what is the one supreme goal? By praising whom, by worshipping whom, can men obtain the good?

5. *Ko dharmaḥ sarva-dharmāṇāṁ*
bhavataḥ paramo mataḥ,
Kiṁ japan mucyate jantur
janma-saṁsāra-bandhanāt.

What duty, of all duties, do you think supreme? By repeating whose name is a creature freed from the bondage of birth and transmigration?

Bhīṣma uvāca:

6. *Jagat-prabhuṁ deva-devam*
anantaṁ puruṣottamam,
Stuvan-nāma-sahasreṇa
puruṣaḥ satatotthitaḥ.

Bhīshma said:
The lord of the world, the god of gods, the infinite, the supreme person — by praising Him constantly by means of His thousand names, a person is always uplifted.

7. *Tam-eva cārcayan nityaṁ*
bhaktyā puruṣam avyayam,
Dhyāyan-stuvan-namasyaṁśca
yajamānas tam-eva ca.

And by worshipping Him alone, constantly with devotion — the imperishable person; by meditation on Him, by praising Him, and by prostrating to Him alone, the worshipper, the aspirant (is freed).

8. *Anādi-nidhanaṁ viṣṇuṁ*
sarva-loka-maheśvaram,
Lokādhyakṣaṁ stuvan nityaṁ
sarva-duḥkhātigo bhavet.

Having neither beginning nor end, Vishnu, the great lord of all the worlds, the witness of the world — by constantly praising Him one can pass beyond all sorrows.

9. *Brahmaṇyaṁ sarva-dharmajñaṁ*
lokānāṁ kīrti-vardhanam,
Loka-nāthaṁ mahad-bhūtaṁ
sarva-bhūta-bhavodbhavam.

The well-wisher of Brahmā, Brāhmins, etc., the knower of all *dharmas,* the enhancer of the fame of men (or the worlds); the lord of the world, the truth absolute, the source of evolution of all things.

10. *Eṣa me sarva-dharmāṇāṁ*
dharmo'dhikatamo mataḥ,
Yad bhaktyā puṇḍarīkākṣaṁ
stavair arcen naraḥ sadā.

This, I think, is the most excellent *dharma* of all *dharmas:* that, with devotion, a man should always glorify the lotus-eyed (Lord) by praises.

11. *Paramaṁ yo mahat-tejaḥ*
paramaṁ yo mahat-tapaḥ,
Paramaṁ yo mahad-brahma
paramaṁ yaḥ parāyaṇam.

He is the supreme great light; He is the supreme great ruler. He is the supreme great Brahman; He is the supreme highest goal.

12. *Pavitrāṇāṁ pavitraṁ yo*
maṅgalānāṁ ca maṅgalam,
Daivataṁ devatānāṁ ca
bhūtānāṁ yo'vyayaḥ pitā.

He is the purest of the pure and the most auspicious of the auspicious and the most divine of divinities. He is the imperishable father of creatures.

13. *Yataḥ sarvāṇi bhūtāni*
bhavanty-ādi-yugāgame,
Yasmiṁśca pralayaṁ yānti
punar-eva yuga-kṣaye.

From Him all creatures proceed in the beginning of an age, and in Him they are absorbed again at the end of the age.

14. *Tasya loka-pradhānasya*
jagan-nāthasya bhūpate,
Viṣṇor-nāma-sahasraṁ me
śṛṇu pāpa-bhayāpaham.

Of that chief of the world, of the lord of the universe, O King (Yudhishthira), of Vishnu, hear from me the thousand names, which remove all sin and fear.

15. *Yāni nāmāni gauṇāni*
vikhyātāni mahātmanaḥ,
Ṛṣibhiḥ parigītāni
tāni vakṣyāmi bhūtaye.

Those famous names of the great soul, which bring out His manifold qualities celebrated by *rishis* (seers), I shall declare for the good (of all).

16. *Ṛṣir nāmnāṁ sahasrasya*
vedavyāso mahā-muniḥ,
Chando'nuṣṭup tathā devo
bhagavān-devakī-sutaḥ.

The *rishi* of the thousand names is Vedavyāsa, the great contemplative sage; the meter is Anushtup; and the deity is the blessed son of Devakī.

17. *Om viṣṇuṁ jiṣṇuṁ mahā-viṣṇuṁ*
prabhaviṣṇuṁ maheśvaram,
Aneka-rūpaṁ daityāntaṁ
namāmi puruṣottamam.

Om. Vishnu, conqueror, great Vishnu, creator, the great Lord, to Him of many forms, the destroyer of demons, to the supreme person, I bow.

Śrī vedavyāsa uvāca:

Om asya śrī-viṣṇor-divya-sahasra-
nāma-stotra-mālā-mantrasya,

Vedavyāsa said:
Om. Of this garland of mantras (constituting) the hymn of praise of the divine thousand names of Vishnu,

Śrī-bhagavān vedavyāsa ṛṣiḥ.

The blessed Vedavyāsa is the seer.

Śrī-kṛṣṇaḥ paramātmā devatā.

Krishna, the supreme Self, is the deity.

Anuṣṭup chandaḥ.

The meter is Anushtup.

Ātma-yoniḥ svayaṁ jāta iti bījam.

"Having His source in the Self, Self-begotten" is the seed.

Devakī-nandanaḥ sraṣṭeti śaktiḥ.

"The son of Devakī, the creator and sustainer" is the power.

Tri-sāmā sāma-gaḥ sāmeti hṛdayam.

"He whose glory is sung in the three types of Sāma songs, the theme of such songs, He who manifests Himself as the *Sāma Veda*" is the heart.

Śaṅkha-bhṛn-nandakī cakrīti kīlakam.

"The bearer of the conch, He of the sword, He of the discus" is the nail.

Śārṅga-dhanvā gadā-dhara ity-astram.

"He of the Shārnga bow, the wielder of the mace" is the weapon.

Rathāṅga-pāṇir-akṣobhya iti kavacam.

"The one holding the reins of a chariot in His hands (Krishna), who is imperturbable" is the armor.

Udbhavaḥ kṣobhaṇo deva iti paramo mantraḥ.

"The source, the vibration, God" is the supreme mantra.

Śrī-mahā-viṣṇu-prīty-arthe
Viṣṇor divya-sahasra-nāma-jape viniyogaḥ.

Let us engage ourselves in the *japa* of the divine thousand names of Vishnu for the purpose of pleasing great Vishnu.

Atha dhyānam.

Now, meditation.

Om śāntākāraṁ bhujaga-śayanaṁ
Padma-nābhaṁ sureśaṁ,

Om. Serene, reclining on the great serpent, having a lotus for His navel, the lord of gods,

Viśvādhāraṁ gagana-sadṛśaṁ
Megha-varṇaṁ śubhāṅgam;

The supporter of the universe, resembling the sky, colored like a cloud, having shapely limbs,

Lakṣmī-kāntaṁ kamala-nayanaṁ
Yogibhir-dhyāna-gamyaṁ,

The lover of Lakshmī, the lotus-eyed, being perceived in meditation by yogīs,

Vande viṣṇuṁ bhava-bhaya-haraṁ
Sarva-lokaika-nātham.

I salute that Vishnu, the remover of the fear of birth, the sole lord of all the worlds.

Om namo bhagavate vāsudevāya.

Om. I bow to the blessed Vāsudeva.

Om namo bhagavate sadāśivāya.

Om. I bow to the blessed Sadāshiva.

Om namo bhagavate muktānandāya.

Om. I bow to the blessed Muktānanda.

VIṢṆU SAHASRANĀMA

The Thousand Names of Vishnu

1. *Om viśvaṁ viṣṇur vaṣaṭkāro*
   bhūta-bhavya-bhavat-prabhuḥ,
   Bhūta-kṛd bhūta-bhṛd bhāvo
   bhūtātmā bhūta-bhāvanaḥ.

Om. Of the form of the universe; entering everything and every being; of the form of *yajña;* lord of past, present, and future; creator of all beings; sustainer of all beings; becoming the universe without losing His nature as pure existence; Self of beings; evolving and nourishing creatures.

2. *Pūtātmā paramātmā ca*
   muktānāṁ paramā gatiḥ,
   Avyayaḥ puruṣaḥ sākṣī
   kṣetrajño'kṣara eva ca.

Pure Self; supreme spirit; ultimate goal of the emancipated; imperishable; person residing in the city of nine gates (body); witness; knower of the field; changeless.

3. *Yogo yoga-vidāṁ netā*
pradhāna-purūṣeśvaraḥ,
Nārasiṁha-vapuḥ śrīmān
keśavaḥ purūṣottamaḥ.

Attainable through yoga; leader of knowers of yoga; master of *prakriti* (nature, matter) and *purusha* (embodied soul); of a half-human and half-lion form; on whose chest Lakshmī (Divine Mother) resides; slayer of the demon Keshī, of beautiful locks of hair; supreme person.

4. *Sarvaḥ śarvaḥ śivaḥ sthāṇur*
bhūtādir nidhir-avyayaḥ,
Sambhavo bhāvano bhartā
prabhavaḥ prabhur īśvaraḥ.

The all; destroyer; free from the three *gunas,* good; motionless, fixed; first cause; unchanging resting place for all beings during dissolution; incarnating; giver of boons; nourisher of all; underlying reality; origin of everything; almighty; ruler of all.

5. *Svayambhūḥ śambhur ādityaḥ*
puṣkarākṣo mahāsvanaḥ,
Anādi-nidhano dhātā
vidhātā dhāturuttamaḥ.

Self-begotten; bestower of good; golden person within the sun; lotus-eyed; of the mighty sound of the Vedas; without birth or death; supporter of the universe; dispenser of the fruits of actions; greater than Brahmā (creator), the subtlest element.

6. *Aprameyo hṛṣīkeśaḥ*
padmanābho'maraprabhuḥ,
Viśvakarmā manus tvaṣṭā
sthaviṣṭhaḥ sthaviro dhruvaḥ.

Indefinable; lord of the senses; from whose navel the cosmic lotus springs; lord of immortals; architect of the universe; thinking being; reducer of all; biggest, supremely gross; primeval and firm.

7. *Agrāhyaḥ śāśvataḥ kṛṣṇo*
lohitākṣaḥ pratardanaḥ,
Prabhūtas trikakubdhāma
pavitraṁ maṅgalaṁ param.

Imperceptible; eternal; dark blue, ground of bliss; red-eyed; bringer of total destruction; ever-full, of the six attributes; foundation of the three realms — above, below, and middle; purifier; supremely auspicious.

8. *Īśānaḥ prāṇadaḥ prāṇo*
jyeṣṭhaḥ śreṣṭhaḥ prajāpatiḥ,
Hiraṇya-garbho bhū-garbho
mādhavo madhu-sūdanaḥ.

Controller of all; giver of life; life of life; oldest; most praiseworthy; master of all living creatures; dweller in the golden cosmic egg; holding the earth in His womb; consort of Lakshmī, realized through silence, meditation, and yoga; slayer of the demon Madhu.

9. *Īśvaro vikramī dhanvī*
medhāvī vikramaḥ kramaḥ,
Anuttamo durādharṣaḥ
kṛtajñaḥ kṛtir ātmavān.

Omnipotent; full of mighty prowess; wielder of the bow; supremely intelligent; riding on the white eagle; measuring the whole world with one step; unequalled; unconquerable by Asuras (demons), however powerful; grateful even for small acts of devotion and worship; dynamic force behind all activities; self-supported.

> 10. *Sureśaḥ śaraṇaṁ śarma*
> *viśva-retāḥ prajābhavaḥ,*
> *Ahaḥ saṁvatsaro vyālaḥ*
> *pratyayaḥ sarvadarśanaḥ.*

God of gods; supreme refuge; infinite bliss; seed of the universe; source of all beings; eternal day; lord of time; difficult to grasp like a serpent; consciousness; all-seeing.

> 11. *Ajaḥ sarveśvaraḥ siddhaḥ*
> *siddhiḥ sarvādir acyutaḥ,*
> *Vṛṣākapir ameyātmā*
> *sarva-yoga-viniḥsṛtaḥ.*

Unborn; sovereign lord of all; eternally perfect; highest attainment; primary cause; infallible; boar who saved the world from unrighteousness; immeasurable; free from all contacts and attachments.

> 12. *Vasur vasumanāḥ satyaḥ*
> *samātmā sammitaḥ samaḥ,*
> *Amoghaḥ puṇḍarīkākṣo*
> *vṛṣakarmā vṛṣākṛtiḥ.*

In whom all beings dwell and who dwells in all; high-minded; unchangeable, ever-existing truth, the real; same in all; easy of access; treating all equally; unfailing; realized in the lotus of the heart; of righteous actions; of the form of *dharmas*.

13. *Rudro bahu-śirā babhrur*
viśvayoniḥ śuci-śravāḥ,
Amṛtaḥ śāśvata-sthāṇur
varāroho mahātapāḥ.

Causing beings to cry; many-headed; supporter of worlds; universal matrix; of pure and sweet names; immortal; everlasting and firm; supreme destination; of infinite knowledge.

14. *Sarvagaḥ sarvavid-bhānur*
viṣvak-seno janārdanaḥ,
Vedo vedavid avyaṅgo
vedāṅgo vedavit kaviḥ.

Going everywhere; omniscient and effulgent; whose mere sight scatters hostile armies; punisher of the wicked and bestower of blessings on the virtuous; giver of knowledge; knower of the Vedas; without imperfections; whose very limbs are the Vedas; spreader of the knowledge of the Vedas; all-seeing.

15. *Lokādhyakṣaḥ surādhyakṣo*
dharmādhyakṣaḥ kṛtākṛtaḥ,
Caturātmā caturvyūhaś
caturdaṁṣṭraś caturbhujaḥ.

Presiding over all worlds; presiding over heavens; witness of righteous as well as unrighteous actions; cause as well as effect; of four fold nature; manifesting into four mighty powers; of four teeth; four-armed.

16. *Bhrājiṣṇur bhojanaṁ bhoktā*
sahiṣṇur jagadādijaḥ,
Anagho vijayo jetā
viśvayoniḥ punarvasuḥ.

Essence of light illuminating everything; food, object of enjoyment; enjoyer, experiencer; subduer of enemies; born in the beginning of the universe; sinless; victorious; excelling all others; sower of seeds in the womb of the universe; residing again and again in bodies.

17. *Upendro vāmanaḥ prāṁśur*
amoghaḥ śucir ūrjitaḥ,
Atīndraḥ saṅgrahaḥ sargo
dhṛtātmā niyamo yamaḥ.

Younger brother of Indra; of dwarfish stature; tallest; whose activities never go to waste; spotlessly clean; infinitely strong and vital; who surpassed Indra; absorbing the entire cosmos into Himself during dissolution; matter; immutable, though ever assuming so many forms; appointing authority; external and internal ruler.

18. *Vedyo vaidyaḥ sadā-yogī*
vīrahā mādhavo madhuḥ,
Atīndriyo mahāmāyo
mahotsāho mahābalaḥ.

Worth knowing; knower of all skills and sciences; eternal yogī; slayer of demoniacal heroes; lord of knowledge; honey of love and bliss; beyond the sense organs; master of *māyā,* the power of illusion; ever-dynamic; stronger than the strong.

19. *Mahā-buddhir mahā-vīryo*
mahā-śaktir mahā-dyutiḥ,
Anirdeśya-vapuḥ śrīmān
ameyātmā mahādri-dhṛk.

Of unlimited wisdom and understanding; cosmic energy; supreme power of manifestation and grace; of splendorous light; of indefinable form; constantly courted by glories; inestimable; supporter of the great mountain.

20. *Maheṣvāso mahībhartā*
śrīnivāsaḥ satāṁ-gatiḥ,
Aniruddhaḥ surānando
govindo govidāṁ patiḥ.

Mighty archer; supporter of the earth; abode of Lakshmī (prosperity, power, glory); the goal of the virtuous; who cannot be deterred or obstructed; giver of joy to gods; master of cows, earth, speech; lord of all knowers of the Veda.

21. *Marīcir damano haṁsaḥ*
suparṇo bhujagottamaḥ,
Hiraṇyanābhaḥ sutapāḥ
padmanābhaḥ prajāpatiḥ.

Supremely lustrous; who chastises and controls; the state of realization of "I am That"; the eagle of beautiful wings; the best of serpents (Shesha); of golden navel; possessing the great power of concentration of mind and control of senses; of lotus-navel; lord of all creatures.

22. *Amṛtyuḥ sarva-dṛk siṁhaḥ*
sandhātā sandhimān sthiraḥ,
Ajo durmarṣaṇaḥ śāstā
viśrutātmā surārihā.

Knowing no decay or death; all-seeing; ferocious lion; bestower of fruits; rejoicing over the fruits which He confers on His devotees; unchanging and stable; moving in the hearts of devotees and throwing away brutal demons; who cannot be endured by His enemies; controlling all by scriptural laws; the supreme Self described in the Vedas; destroyer of the enemies of celestials.

23. *Gurur gurutamo dhāma*
satyaḥ satya-parākramaḥ,
Nimiṣo'nimiṣaḥ sragvī
vācaspatir-udāra-dhīḥ.

First teacher; greatest teacher, the teacher of Brahmā (the creator); final abode; greatest speaker of truth; of true valor; with closed eyes; always wide awake; always wearing the Vaijayantī garland, which represents the five elements in their gross and subtle forms; master of all sciences and of vast intellect.

24. *Agraṇīr grāmaṇīḥ śrīmān*
nyāyo netā samīraṇaḥ,
Sahasra-mūrdhā viśvātmā
sahasrākṣaḥ sahasrapāt.

Lifting aspirants to the highest liberation; director of beings; of unsurpassable loveliness and grandeur; justice, logic, and reason; plying the cosmic wheel of evolution; cause of every movement in the world; with a thousand (uncountable) heads; soul of the universe; with a thousand eyes; with a thousand feet.

25. *Āvartano nivṛttātmā*
saṁvṛtaḥ sampramardanaḥ,
Ahaḥsaṁvartako vahnir
anilo dharaṇīdharaḥ.

Turner of the cosmic wheel; transcendental being free of all identifications; veiled by *māyā;* annihilator of all; sun god who regulates days; fire, carrying oblations to gods; homeless, breathing perpetually as air; bearer of earth.

26. *Suprasādaḥ prasannātmā*
viśvadhṛg viśvabhug vibhuḥ,
Satkartā satkṛtaḥ sādhur
jahnur nārāyaṇo naraḥ.

Bestowing grace liberally; ever-pure and cheerful; subduer and conqueror of all; protecting and enjoying all; manifesting in an endless variety of forms; honoring the good and wise; honored and adored by the good and wise; of righteous actions; abandoning all those lacking in devotion and wisdom; sole refuge for embodied beings; guide, leader.

27. *Asaṅkhyeyo'prameyātmā*
viśiṣṭaḥ śiṣṭa-kṛc chuciḥ,
Siddhārthaḥ siddhasaṅkalpaḥ
siddhidaḥ siddhisādhanaḥ.

Of countless names and forms; imperceptible; unique; law giver; immaculate; who has gained all there is to gain; accomplishing immediately whatever He wills; fulfiller of desires, giver of powers; means for all achievements.

28. *Vṛṣāhī vṛṣabho viṣṇur*
vṛṣaparvā vṛṣodaraḥ,
Vardhano vardhamānaśca
viviktaḥ śruti-sāgaraḥ.

Possessing offerings made in rituals; showering blessings on devotees; who measured the entire universe in three strides; steps in the ladder to the ultimate reality; holding all beings in His belly during dissolution; nourisher of all; expanding Himself to any dimensions; alone, unaffected; ocean of the Vedas.

29. *Subhujo durdharo vāgmī*
mahendro vasudo vasuḥ,
Naika-rūpo bṛhad-rūpaḥ
śipiviṣṭaḥ prākaśanaḥ.

Of graceful, long arms; whom the yogīs find difficult to locate in their hearts during meditation; from whom speech issues; lord of Indra; liberal giver of wealth; wealth; myriad-formed; of infinite dimensions; source of luminous rays; illuminator of all.

30. *Ojas-tejo-dyutidharaḥ*
prakāśātmā pratāpanaḥ,
Ṛddhaḥ spaṣṭākṣaro mantraś
candrāṁśur bhāskara-dyutiḥ.

Possessor of strength, majesty, and luminosity; self-effulgent; diffuser of heat and light; rich in knowledge, detachment, *dharma;* clear and imperishable sound Om; progenitor and goal of Vedic mantras; cool and nourishing moon rays; resplendent sun.

31. *Amṛtāṁśūdbhavo bhānuḥ*
śaśabinduḥ sureśvaraḥ,
Auṣadhaṁ jagataḥ setuḥ
satya-dharma-parākramaḥ.

Source of the nectarine moon; shining gloriously; nourishing all plants and herbs as the moon; god of gods; sole medicine for the disease of becoming; the bridge for crossing the ocean of mundane existence; employing His prowess for truth and righteousness.

32. *Bhūta-bhavya-bhavan-nāthaḥ*
pavanaḥ pāvano'nalaḥ,
Kāmahā kāmakṛt kāntaḥ
kāmaḥ kāmapradaḥ prabhuḥ.

Lord and refuge of all past, present, and future beings; great purifier; causing the wind to blow; sustaining life as fire; destroyer of desires; fulfiller of desires; enchantingly lovely; supreme beloved; granting all desires; supreme in all respects.

33. *Yugādi-kṛd yugāvarto*
naikamāyo mahāśanaḥ,
Adṛśyo vyaktarūpaśca
sahasrajid anantajit.

Originator of eons; turning the eons; having many *māyās* (powers) with which He carries on the cosmic creation; most voracious eater, who swallows up all creatures during dissolution; ungraspable by the mind and the senses; with a tangible form; vanquisher of thousands of demons; conqueror of countless beings.

34. *Iṣṭo viśiṣṭaḥ śiṣṭeṣṭaḥ*
śikhaṇḍī nahuṣo vṛṣaḥ,
Krodhahā krodhakṛt-kartā
viśvabāhur mahīdharaḥ.

Dear to all, object of adoration; loving all equally; especially dear to the *jñānīs;* wearing a peacock feather; binding creatures by His *māyā;* showerer of blessings, incarnation of *dharma;* dispelling anger from all seekers; assuming anger while dealing with the wicked; with arms on all sides; substratum and support of the earth.

35. *Acyutaḥ prathitaḥ prāṇaḥ*
prāṇado vāsavānujaḥ,
Apāṁ-nidhir adhiṣṭhānaṁ
apramattaḥ pratiṣṭhitaḥ.

Changeless; whose glory has spread everywhere; sustainer of *prāna;* giving life and strength to gods and death to demons; younger brother of Indra; treasury of waters — ocean; ground of the cosmos; never forgetful or inattentive or committing a mistake; supported by His own greatness.

36. *Skandaḥ skandadharo dhuryo*
varado vāyuvāhanaḥ,
Vāsudevo bṛhad-bhānur
ādidevaḥ purandaraḥ.

Commander-in-chief of the celestial army; upholder of *dharma;* sustainer of the cosmic burden; granter of boons; supporter of the seven great winds; who is in everything and in whom everything lives; whose rays are the sun and the moon; primary cosmic cause; destroyer of the cities or bodies of demons.

37. *Aśokas tāraṇas tāraḥ*
śūraḥ śaurir janeśvaraḥ,
Anukūlaḥ śatāvartaḥ
padmī padmanibhekṣaṇaḥ.

Devoid of sorrow; enabling seekers to cross the ocean of change; savior (from the fears of birth, old age, and death); valiant; son of Vasudeva; Lord of men; friend and well-wisher of all; taking one hundred (innumerable) incarnations for establishing *dharma;* bearer of a lotus in His hand; lotus-eyed.

38. *Padmanābho'ravindākṣaḥ*
padmagarbhaḥ śarīrabhṛt,
Mahardhir ṛddho vṛddhātmā
mahākṣo garuḍadhvajaḥ.

Center of the cosmic lotus; lotus-eyed (Krishna); dwelling in the heart lotus; sustainer of the body; of glorious wealth and unquestionable sovereignty; who has expanded Himself to be the universe; ancient Self; great-eyed; having the eagle as His insignia on His flag.

39. *Atulaḥ śarabho bhīmaḥ*
samayajño havirhariḥ,
Sarvalakṣaṇalakṣaṇyo
lakṣmīvān samitiñjayaḥ.

Unrivaled; luminous Self—all bodies; terrible; knower of the reality of time, whose best worship is the vision of equality; receiver of oblations; known through different methods of inquiry; consort of Lakshmī; ever-victorious.

40. *Vikṣaro rohito mārgo*
hetur dāmodaraḥ sahaḥ,
Mahīdharo mahābhāgo
vegavān amitāśanaḥ.

Undecaying; red-complexioned, who incarnated as a fish; the way; material and instrumental cause of everything; who was tied by Yashodā with a cord round His waist; all-enduring; supporter of the earth; ever-fortunate; exceedingly swift; of insatiable appetite.

41. *Udbhavaḥ kṣobhaṇo devaḥ*
śrīgarbhaḥ parameśvaraḥ,
Karaṇaṁ kāraṇaṁ kartā
vikartā gahano guhaḥ.

Originator; stirring primordial matter; sporting with creation; having the cosmos within Him before and after creation; greatest Lord; instrumental cause; material cause; doer; creator of endless varieties; hidden from view; concealing Himself by His own power.

42. *Vyavasāyo vyavasthānaḥ*
saṁsthānaḥ sthānado dhruvaḥ,
Pararddhiḥ paramaspaṣṭas
tuṣṭaḥ puṣṭaḥ śubhekṣaṇaḥ.

Resolute and persevering; governing the universe in an orderly manner; absorber of all; conferring states or positions on devotees; fixed and constant; possessor of the greatest majesty and possessions; exceedingly vivid; ever-contented; ever-full; of auspicious and lovely glance.

43. *Rāmo virāmo virato*
mārgo neyo nayo'nayaḥ,
Vīraḥ śaktimatāṁ śreṣṭho
dharmo dharmaviduttamaḥ.

In whom the yogīs revel, who incarnated as Rāma; abode of perfect rest; passionless; path of salvation; guide; leader; without leader or commander; heroic warrior; mightiest of the mighty; law of being; greatest knower of *dharma.*

44. *Vaikuṇṭhaḥ puruṣaḥ prāṇaḥ*
prāṇadaḥ praṇavaḥ pṛthuḥ,
Hiraṇyagarbhaḥ śatrughno
vyāpto vāyur adhokṣajaḥ.

Uniter of elements; consuming all sins; life-breath of all beings; giver and taker of life; Om, that which is praised and adored by gods; King Prithu; the golden egg out of which Brahmā was born; destroyer of enemies; all-pervasive; creator of fragrance, life-giving power in the air; whose vital fluid never flows downward.

45. *Ṛtuḥ sudarśanaḥ kālaḥ*
parameṣṭhī parigrahaḥ,
Ugraḥ saṁvatsaro dakṣo
viśrāmo viśva-dakṣiṇaḥ.

Lord of seasons; whose glimpse is auspicious, of beautiful eyes; time which counts everything; centered in His own infinite glory; receiving devotees' offerings gladly and readily; terrible, of whom even the sun, wind, and fire are frightened; abode of all beings; clever and quick; resting place; the most skillful and efficient.

46. *Vistāraḥ sthāvara-sthāṇuḥ*
pramāṇaṁ bījamavyayam,
Artho'nartho mahākośo
mahābhogo mahādhanaḥ.

Extending Himself limitlessly; firm and motionless; proof of everything; immutable seed; being most pleasing and delightful, He is desired by all; whose every desire has been fulfilled; wrapped in great sheaths; most delightful to enjoy; supremely wealthy.

47. *Anirviṇṇaḥ sthaviṣṭho'bhūr*
dharma-yūpo mahāmakhaḥ,
Nakṣatranemir nakṣatrī
kṣamaḥ kṣāmaḥ samīhanaḥ.

Unwearied, unapathetic; with a gross cosmic form; birthless; the post to which all *dharmas* are tied; great sacrifice; nave of stars and planets; the moon, lord of stars; patient as the earth; surviving even when all others perish in the final deluge; of benevolent desires.

48. *Yajña ijyo mahejyaśca*
kratuḥ satraṁ satāṁ-gatiḥ,
Sarvadarśī vimuktātmā
sarvajño jñānamuttamam.

Sacrifice; goal of sacrifice; supreme object of worship; sacrificial post; the sacrifice to which learned men are called; destination of the good; all-knowing; ever-free; omniscient; highest wisdom.

49. *Suvrataḥ sumukhaḥ sūkṣmaḥ*
sughoṣaḥ sukhadaḥ suhṛt,
Manoharo jita-krodho
vīrabāhur vidāraṇaḥ.

Of the pure vow—that He will save anyone who turns to Him; of enchanting face; subtlest of the subtle; of auspicious

Vedic sounds; giving happiness to the noble and taking away joy from the vicious; disinterested friend; fascinating; conqueror of anger and other passions; valiant-armed; tearer of diabolical creatures.

50. *Svāpanaḥ svavaśo vyāpī*
naikātmā naikakarmakṛt,
Vatsaro vatsalo vatsī
ratnagarbho dhaneśvaraḥ.

Putting all beings to sleep by His *māyā;* His own master; all-pervading; becoming many; performing numerous functions; abode of all; supremely affectionate; universal father; womb of jewels, ocean; lord of boundless wealth.

51. *Dharmagub dharmakṛd dharmī*
sad asat kṣaram akṣaram,
Avijñātā sahasrāṁśur
vidhātā kṛtalakṣaṇaḥ.

Protector of *dharma;* of righteous deeds; seer of *dharma;* unchanging and absolute; unreal, limited; perishable; imperishable; nonknower; thousand-rayed; arbiter of destiny; author of all scriptures.

52. *Gabhastinemiḥ sattvasthaḥ*
siṁho bhūtamaheśvaraḥ,
Ādidevo mahādevo
deveśo devabhṛd-guruḥ.

Light of lights; abiding in the *sattva guna* (purity and radiance); brave as a lion; mighty Lord of beings; primal deity; supreme being; master of gods; preceptor of Indra, the king of gods.

53. *Uttaro gopatir goptā*
jñānagamyaḥ purātanaḥ,
Śarīra-bhūtabhṛd bhoktā
kapīndro bhūridakṣiṇaḥ.

Who lifts us from the ocean of worldliness; master of cows, speech, earth, senses; protector of all; attainable through knowledge; most ancient; nourisher of the five elements of which the body is made; experiencer; Rāma, the lord of monkeys; bestower of liberal gifts.

54. *Somapo'mṛtapaḥ somaḥ*
purujit purusattamaḥ,
Vinayo jayaḥ satyasandho
dāśārhaḥ sāttvatāṁ-patiḥ.

Who drinks the Soma juice offered in sacrifices; enjoyer of His own immortal, nectarine bliss; nourishing the plants as the moon; conqueror of hordes of enemies; omnipresent and the greatest; punisher of evildoers; victory incarnate; whose resolves are always fulfilled; born in the Dashārha race (Krishna); Lord of the followers of the *sāttvata* (sattvic) branch of Tantra.

55. *Jīvo vinayitā-sākṣī*
mukundo'mitavikramaḥ,
Ambhonidhir anantātmā
mahodadhiśayo'ntakaḥ.

Embodied being; witness of the change in His devotees from pride to humility; bestower of salvation; of immeasurable prowess; ocean; beyond the limitations of space, time, and substance; who lies on the great ocean during the deluge; death, mutability.

56. *Ajo mahārhaḥ svābhāvyo*
jitāmitraḥ pramodanaḥ,
Ānando nandano nandaḥ
satyadharmā trivikramaḥ.

Lord of love, boon of Vishnu; worthy of highest worship; of immutable nature; conqueror of internal and external enemies; constant enjoyer of His own eternal, blissful nature; unbounded, pure bliss; bestower of bliss; who has transcended sensuous, limited pleasures; with unchangeable qualities of wisdom, bliss, etc.; who covered the three worlds with three steps.

57. *Maharṣiḥ-kapilācāryaḥ*
kṛtajño medinīpatiḥ,
Tripadas tridaśādhyakṣo
mahāśṛṅgaḥ kṛtāntakṛt.

Who manifested as the great sage Kapila, the founder of the Sānkhya system; the universe and its soul; Lord of the earth; three-lettered Aum; master and witness of the three states of waking, dream, and deep sleep; with a huge horn (in His fish incarnation); destroyer of death.

58. *Mahāvarāho govindaḥ*
suṣeṇaḥ kanakāṅgadī,
Guhyo gabhīro gahano
guptaś cakragadādharaḥ.

Great boar; who is known through the Vedas; with an army of angels to carry on His work; wearing golden armlets; hidden in the heart cave; unfathomable; impenetrable; concealed deep inside; bearer of the discus and the mace.

59. *Vedhāḥ svāṅgo'jitaḥ kṛṣṇo*
dṛḍhaḥ saṅkarṣaṇo'cyutaḥ,
Varuṇo vāruṇo vṛkṣaḥ
puṣkarākṣo mahāmanāḥ.

Universal parent and guide; accomplishing all tasks by Himself, without external aids; invincible; who incarnated as Krishna Dvaipāyana (full name of Vyāsa); firmly retaining His divine powers in their fullness in spite of descending to the earth in various incarnations; absorbing the cosmos into Himself without falling away from His own essential nature; setting sun; son of Varuna (either of the two great seers, Vasishtha or Agastya); the cosmic tree (the Ashvattha tree of the *Bhagavad Gītā*); filling all space; of vast mind.

60. *Bhagavān bhagahā nandī*
vanamālī halāyudhaḥ,
Āditya jyotirādityaḥ
sahiṣṇur gatisattamaḥ.

Having the six great glories—*dharma,* wealth, sovereignty, fame, dispassion, and freedom; destroyer of the world during dissolution; absolute bliss; wearing the Vaijayantī garland of forest flowers; wielding the plough as His weapon in His incarnation as Balabhadra, Krishna's brother; the son of Aditi in His incarnation as Vāmana (the dwarf); the resplendent greater sun, residing within the solar orb; enduring pairs of opposites such as heat and cold; highest goal.

61. *Sudhanvā khaṇḍaparaśur*
dāruṇo draviṇapradaḥ,
Diva-spṛk sarvadṛg-vyāso
vācaspatir-ayonijaḥ.

Bearer of the auspicious Shārnga bow; wielding the great axe in His incarnation as Parashurāma; merciless toward the unrighteous; liberal giver of wealth; touching the sky in His universal form revealed to Arjuna; great Vyāsa, who saw all truths and arranged all knowledge into the Vedas, Purānas, and *Brahma Sūtras;* the unborn lord of knowledge.

62. *Trisāmā sāmagaḥ sāma*
nirvāṇaṁ bheṣajaṁ bhiṣak,
Sannyāsakṛc chamaḥ śānto
niṣṭhā śāntiḥ parāyaṇam.

Glorified by the three kinds of Sāma songs (occurring in the *Sāma Veda*); singer of Sāma songs; *Sāma Veda;* the goal of deliverance from sorrow; unfailing remedy for the disease of becoming; divine physician who taught the science of the absolute in the *Gītā;* institutor of *sannyāsa* (total renunciation); subduer of all unruly passions; unattached to pleasure, unperturbed; in whom all creatures rest in dead silence during dissolution; whose very nature is peace; having attained whom one never returns.

63. *Śubhāṅgaḥ śāntidaḥ sraṣṭā*
kumudaḥ kuvaleśayaḥ,
Gohito gopatir goptā
vṛṣabhākṣo vṛṣapriyaḥ.

Of the most beautiful form; giver of peace, free from attachment and aversion; creator of embodied beings; rejoicing in His creation; lying on the couch of the serpent Shesha, floating in the ocean surrounding the earth; lover and savior of cows and the earth; husband of the earth; who conceals Himself in His creations by His power of *māyā;* whose eyes are *dharma* itself, raining the desired fruits on the righteous; who delights in *dharma.*

64. *Anivartī nivṛttātmā*
saṅkṣeptā kṣemakṛc chivaḥ,
Śrīvatsavakṣāḥ śrīvāsaḥ
śrīpatiḥ śrīmatāṁ-varaḥ.

Who never knows retreat; detached from pleasures and enjoyments; who gathers the wide world into Himself at the time of dissolution; who protects devotees by enabling them to preserve securely what they have gained; who purifies an aspirant by the very thought of His name; having the sacred Shrīvatsa mark (the mark of the sage Bhrigu's foot) on His chest; whose bosom is the eternal abode of Lakshmī; who was chosen by Lakshmī to be Her beloved husband; greatest master of the *Rig, Yajur,* and *Sāma Vedas.*

65. *Śrīdaḥ śrīśaḥ śrīnivāsaḥ*
śrīnidhiḥ śrīvibhāvanaḥ,
Śrīdharaḥ śrīkaraḥ śreyaḥ
śrīmāṁl-lokatrayāśrayah.

Giver of wealth and glory; lord of Lakshmī, the goddess of success, wealth, and glory; who dwells and manifests in good people; treasure house of all energies; who confers wealth and glory on people according to their accumulated merit; always bearing Lakshmī, the mother of all beings, in His bosom; bestower of wealth and fame on His devotees; the highest good — liberation; possessor of all riches and powers; shelter for the three worlds.

66. *Svakṣaḥ svaṅgaḥ śatānando*
nandir jyotirgaṇeśvaraḥ,
Vijitātmā vidheyātmā
satkīrtiś chinnasaṁśayaḥ.

With beautiful eyes; with captivating limbs; whose bliss is immeasurable, creatures enjoying only a fraction of it; of the nature of infinite bliss; lord of all luminous bodies; with complete control over His mind; under nobody else's control; of true fame; beyond doubts, dispeller of doubts.

67. *Udīrṇaḥ sarvataścakṣur*
anīśaḥ śāśvataḥ sthiraḥ,
Bhūśayo bhūṣaṇo bhūtir
viśokaḥ śokanāśanaḥ.

Who surpasses everyone; with eyes on all sides; with none to rule over Him; eternal and immutable; resting on the ground in His Rāma incarnation; who adorns the world; pure existence; without sorrow; destroyer of sorrow.

68. *Arciṣmān arcitaḥ kumbho*
viśuddhātmā viśodhanaḥ,
Aniruddho'pratirathaḥ
pradyumno'mitavikramaḥ.

Source of all effulgence; worshipped even by Brahmā and others; the primordial pot in which all powers and deities are established; the absolutely pure Self; supreme purifier; who cannot be vanquished by any opponent; without an enemy who could stand against Him; possessor of limitless wealth; of unbounded might.

69. *Kālaneminihā vīraḥ*
śauriḥ śūrajaneśvaraḥ,
Trilokātmā trilokeśaḥ
keśavaḥ keśihā hariḥ.

Slayer of the demon Kālanemi (Time); most valiant warrior; born in the Shūra clan; who overcomes great warriors by His extraordinary prowess and rules them; the innermost reality of the three worlds; governor of the three worlds; whose long hairs are the rays which illumine the sun; slayer of the demon Keshī; annihilator of the ills of the world.

70. *Kāmadevaḥ kāmapālaḥ*
kāmī kāntaḥ kṛtāgamaḥ,
Anirdeśyavapur viṣṇur
vīro'nanto dhanañjayaḥ.

Whom the people worship for the fulfillment of their four aspirations; fulfiller of the desires of His devotees; completely fulfilled; of ravishing beauty; author of the scriptures; whose light fills all space and even goes beyond; with characteristics of quick motion, existence, radiance, etc. (implied by the root *vi*); endless; Arjuna, who conquered kingdoms and gained vast wealth.

71. *Brahmaṇyo brahmakṛd brahmā*
brahma brahmavivardhanaḥ,
Brahmavid brāhmaṇo brahmī
brahmajño brāhmaṇapriyaḥ.

Patron of the Vedas, Brāhmins, austerities, and knowledge; author of all these; creator of all; true knowledge which dispels all differences and duality; promotor of the Vedas, austerities, righteousness, etc.; knower of the Vedas; disseminating Vedic knowledge through Brāhmins who are dedicated to the Vedas; whose glory is enhanced by Brahman (Vedas, austerities, etc.); knower of His own absolute nature, who is dear to Brāhmins and to whom they are dear.

72. *Mahākramo mahākarmā*
mahātejā mahoragaḥ,
Mahākratur mahāyajvā
mahāyajño mahāhaviḥ.

Of immeasurably long strides; performer of great deeds; by whose light the sun is fed with light and shines; the great serpent Shesha upon which Lord Vishnu reclines; great sacrifice (Ashvamedha Yajña); performer of great sacrifices; *japa*—sacrifice; great offering.

73. *Stavyaḥ stavapriyaḥ stotraṁ*
stutiḥ stotā raṇapriyaḥ,
Pūrṇaḥ pūrayitā puṇyaḥ
puṇyakīrtir anāmayaḥ.

Great object of praise; pleased by sincere praise and prayer; song of praise; act of praise; praiser, adorer; lover of battles; full of everything that could be wished for by anyone; making His devotees full like Himself; fountain of purity; of pure and fully merited fame; untouched by any physical or mental ailments.

74. *Manojavas tīrthakaro*
vasuretā vasupradaḥ,
Vasuprado vāsudevo
vasur vasumanā haviḥ.

As swift as thought; founder of the fourteen auxiliary sciences; with golden vital fluid; munificent giver of material wealth; giver of the wealth of salvation; son of Vasudeva (Krishna); who resides in the hearts of all beings and in whose heart all beings reside; redeemer of all beings, great and small; oblation.

75. *Sadgatiḥ satkṛtiḥ sattā*
sadbhūtiḥ satparāyaṇaḥ,
Śūraseno yaduśreṣṭhaḥ
sannivāsaḥ suyāmunaḥ.

The goal of good and noble seekers; of great, benevolent deeds; pure, absolute existence; eternal, supremely intelligent, shining and unchanging Self; cherished destination of the knowers of Truth; having armies of valiant warriors like Hanumān, Arjuna, Bhīma, etc.; the foremost in the clan of Yadus (Krishna); abode of the pure-hearted; loved by the righteous people living on the banks of the Yamunā (Krishna).

76. *Bhūtāvāso vāsudevaḥ*
sarvāsunilayo'nalaḥ,
Darpahā darpado dṛpto
durdharo'thāparājitaḥ.

Dwelling place of all beings; covering the cosmos with His *māyā;* abode of all life energies; of limitless glory and power; subduer of pride; giver of pride; ever drunk with His own bliss; difficult to concentrate on; unvanquished.

77. *Viśvamūrtir mahāmūrtir*
dīptamūrtir amūrtimān,
Anekamūrtir avyaktaḥ
śatamūrtiḥ śatānanaḥ.

Of universal form; reclining upon the Shesha couch in His celestial form; of resplendent form; formless; multiformed; unmanifest; of myriad forms; of countless faces.

78. *Eko naikaḥ savaḥ kaḥ kiṁ*
yat tat padamanuttamam,
Lokabandhur lokanātho
mādhavo bhaktavatsalaḥ.

One without a second; exhibiting Himself as many; of the nature of the Soma sacrifice in which Soma juice is extracted and later drunk; supreme happiness; the sole object of inquiry by all yogīs and *jñānīs;* that which is self-existent; indicated by That; unequalled state of perfection; friend of all; solicited by all; born in the family of Madhu; full of boundless love for His devotees.

79. *Suvarṇavarṇo hemāṅgo*
varāṅgaś candanāṅgadī,
Vīrahā viṣamaḥ śūnyo
ghṛtāśīr acalaś calaḥ.

Gold-complexioned; with golden body and limbs; with beautiful, well-proportioned form; adorned with lovely armlets; slayer of heroes on the enemy side; unequalled; void, without attributes; totally devoid of any want; unmoving; of unchangeable nature; constantly moving as the wind.

80. *Amānī mānado mānyo*
lokasvāmī trilokadhṛk,
Sumedhā medhajo dhanyaḥ
satyamedhā dharādharaḥ.

Free of vanity, never confusing not-Self with Self; giver of honor, causing by His *māyā* false identification with not-Self; worthy of greatest honor; master of all the fourteen worlds; supporter of the three worlds; of bright and pure intelligence; who reveals Himself in sacrifices by His grace; supremely fortunate; whose intelligence never fails; as Shesha, bearer and supporter of the earth.

81. *Tejovṛṣo dyutidharaḥ*
sarvaśastrabhṛtāṁ varaḥ,
Pragraho nigraho vyagro
naikaśṛṅgo gadāgrajaḥ.

Who produces clouds by the rays of His sun and pours down rain; bearing a splendid, effulgent form; best of those who wield weapons (greatest warrior); who accepts with satisfaction the offerings made by devotees, who controls the uncontrollable steeds of sense organs; controlling the entire cosmos by His power; always intent on fulfilling His devotees' desires; many-horned (four-horned bull of the Vedas); invoked through mantras.

82. *Caturmūrtiś caturbāhuś*
caturvyūhaś caturgatiḥ,
Caturātmā caturbhāvaś
caturvedavid ekapāt.

Four-formed; four-armed; having four manifestations; the final destination of the seekers of all four castes; with four inner organs—mind, intellect, ego, and memory; from whom the four aspirations—*dharma, artha, kāma,* and *moksha* — are derived; fully conversant with the four Vedas; of whose power the whole cosmos is a mere fraction.

83. *Samāvarto nivṛttātmā*
durjayo duratikramaḥ,
Durlabho durgamo durgo
durāvāso durārihā.

Turning the cosmic wheel efficiently; moving the entire cosmos without moving Himself; unconquerable; whose commands cannot be transgressed even by great gods such as Sun, Fire, Indra, Death, etc.; unattainable without devotion; difficult to comprehend; not easily accessible to the wicked; whom the yogīs lodge in their hearts with great difficulty; slayer of mighty armies of demons.

84. *Śubhāṅgo lokasāraṅgaḥ*
sutantus tantuvardhanaḥ,
Indrakarmā mahākarmā
kṛtakarmā kṛtāgamaḥ.

Of graceful limbs; easily accessible through the repetition of Om, which is the essence of the world; emanating from His own being fine cosmic threads; expanding and destroying the universe; ruling the entire cosmos; whose deeds are mighty; whose deeds are meant for the evolution of embodied souls; author of the Vedas.

85. *Udbhavaḥ sundaraḥ sundo*
ratnanābhaḥ sulocanaḥ,
Arko vājasanaḥ śṛṅgī
jayantaḥ sarvavij-jayī.

Of glorious births (incarnations); of unsurpassed beauty; whose heart is always wet with compassion; of fascinating navel; of enchanting eyes; worshipped even by those whom the world worships; bountiful giver of food; with one horn in the fish incarnation; whose blessings bestow all riches and successes; omniscient and conqueror of all internal and external enemies.

86. *Suvarṇabindur akṣobhyaḥ*
sarvavāgīśvareśvaraḥ,
Mahāhrado mahāgarto
mahābhūto mahānidhiḥ.

Whose celestial form shines like gold in every particle; unshaken by passions or temptations; greatest master of all speech; cool pool of bliss; whose *māyā* is a bottomless abyss; great being, beyond time; treasure house of all souls.

87. *Kumudaḥ kundaraḥ kundaḥ*
parjanyaḥ pāvano'nilaḥ,
Amṛtāśo'mṛtavapuḥ
sarvajñaḥ sarvatomukhaḥ.

Who gladdens the earth by relieving her of her burden of sinners; who tore the earth in the boar incarnation; as captivating as a *kunda* flower; who showers grace to allay the scorching heat of worldliness; greatest purifier of all who remember Him; who never sleeps, who reveals Himself to His devotees in visions; immortal nectar; of immortal body; knower of everything; having faces on all sides.

88. *Sulabhaḥ suvrataḥ siddhaḥ*
śatrujic chatrutāpanaḥ,
Nyagrodho'dumbaro'śvatthaś
cāṇūrāndhra-niṣūdanaḥ.

Whom it is easy to please; fasting and feasting properly in accordance with His vows; whose greatness and glory are His own, not derived from others; ever-triumphant over enemies; scorcher of enemies; who rises and lives over the top of the entire cosmos; transcending the sky; tree of life, the Ashvattha tree, slayer of Chānūra, a mighty wrestler.

89. *Sahasrārciḥ saptajihvaḥ*
saptaidhāḥ saptavāhanaḥ,
Amūrtir anagho'cintyo
bhayakṛd bhayanāśanaḥ.

Emanating innumerable dazzling rays; seven-tongued god of fire; the sacred fire into which seven sticks are thrown ceremonially; sun god riding in His chariot drawn by seven horses; totally devoid of subtle and gross matter; painless and sinless; incomprehensible to the mind and intellect; striking terror in the hearts of the vicious; exterminator of fear.

90. *Aṇur bṛhad kṛśaḥ sthūlo*
guṇabhṛn nirguṇo mahān,
Adhṛtaḥ svadhṛtaḥ svāsyaḥ
prāgvaṁśo vaṁśavardhanaḥ.

Subtlest; greatest; slim and delicate; grossest; assuming three *gunas* for creation, sustenance, and dissolution; devoid of attributes; of the highest glory; who supports all but is supported by none; self-supported; of effulgent, auspicious face; of the most ancient ancestry; who multiplies His descendants (creatures).

91. *Bhārabhṛt kathito yogī*
yogīśaḥ sarvakāmadaḥ,
Āśramaḥ śramaṇaḥ kṣāmaḥ
suparṇo vāyuvāhanaḥ.

Bearing the cosmic burden; who is declared to be the highest goal by the Vedas; realizable through yoga; king of yogīs; granter of all desired fruits; resting place for those tossed about by the storms of life; chastiser of those groveling in ignorance; who reduces persistent sinners to miserable straits; in whom is rooted the *samsāra* tree with Vedas as its leaves; by whose command winds blow.

92. *Dhanurdharo dhanurvedo*
daṇḍo damayitā damaḥ,
Aparājitaḥ sarvasaho
niyantā niyamo yamaḥ.

Always carrying a mighty bow in the Rāma incarnation; unexcelled master of the science of archery; punisher of the wicked; who, as Yama and other deities, purges sinners by punishment; punishment which reforms wrongdoers; ever-unvanquished; with the power to accomplish any task He takes up; controller of all subsidiary cosmic functionaries; who is under the control of none; who knows no death.

93. *Sattvavān sāttvikaḥ satyaḥ*
satyadharma-parāyaṇaḥ,
Abhiprāyaḥ priyārho'rhaḥ
priyakṛt prītivardhanaḥ.

Having heroic courage and strength; mainly established in the *sattva guna;* extremely good to holy beings; unshakably devoted to truth and *dharma;* sought after earnestly by those who want to realize all of the four goals; who is worthy of being given what is valuable and dear to one's heart; deserving all the different modes of worship described in the scriptures; who honors and extols His devoted worshippers; who releases more and more love and devotion in His devotees' hearts.

94. *Vihāyasagatir jyotiḥ*
surucir hutabhug vibhuḥ,
Ravir virocanaḥ sūryaḥ
savitā ravilocanaḥ.

Having His abode in the sky; self-illumined; whose desires and tastes are combined with benevolence and grace; real enjoyer of all oblations offered to different deities; present everywhere; who, as the sun, absorbs vapors from the earth below; dear in different ways to different devotees; who, as the sun, generates various kinds of wealth; father of all; having the sun for His eye.

95. *Ananto hutabhug bhoktā*
sukhado naikajo'grajaḥ,
Anirviṇṇaḥ sadāmarṣī
lokādhiṣṭhānam adbhutaḥ.

Unlimited by space and time; consumer of oblations; enjoyer of the world; who wards off difficulties and pains coming to His devotees; taking many births for the sake of humanity; first to appear in the cosmos; who never suffers any disappointment or dejection; ever ready to forgive trespasses; sole substratum of the universe, animate and inanimate; ever an object of wonder.

96. *Sanāt sanātanatamaḥ*
kapilaḥ kapir avyayaḥ,
Svastidaḥ svastikṛt svasti
svastibhuk svastidakṣiṇaḥ.

Unlimited by time as time issues from Him; most ancient; of yellow color resembling the color of the all-consuming conflagration; who drinks off vapors from the earth (sun); indestructible resting place; bestower of blessings; ever active for the welfare of His devotees; auspiciousness, bliss incarnate; enjoyer of blessings; who bestows blessings deftly.

97. *Araudraḥ kuṇḍalī cakrī*
vikramy-ūrjitaśāsanaḥ,
Śabdātigaḥ śabdasahaḥ
śiśiraḥ śarvarīkaraḥ.

Without fierce actions, wishes, or dislikes; wearing earrings (Sānkhya and Yoga) as brilliant as the sun; bearer of the Sudarshana Chakra (the auspicious circular weapon); of most heroic valor; whose commandments cannot be violated; transcending all words; amenable to indirect verbal descriptions; cool lake for those burned by worldly torments; creator of darkness.

98. *Akrūraḥ peśalo dakṣo*
dakṣiṇaḥ kṣamiṇāṁ-varaḥ,
Vidvattamo vītabhayaḥ
puṇyaśravaṇakīrtanaḥ.

Never getting furious or brutal; friendly and soft in all His actions, thoughts, and words; acting promptly and efficiently; bountiful giver; excelling all others in patience and endurance; greatest of the wise; totally free from fear; whose names, if heard and sung, bring the highest good.

99. *Uttāraṇo duṣkṛtihā*
puṇyo duḥsvapna-nāśanaḥ,
Vīrahā rakṣaṇaḥ santo
jīvanaḥ paryavasthitaḥ.

Lifting aspirants out of the ocean of change; destroyer of sins and hopeless sinners; teaching through scriptures how to acquire merit; dispeller of bad dreams; who puts an end to the cycle of birth and death; protector of the three worlds; manifesting His glory through the righteous; life of all beings; filling the entire cosmos.

100. *Ananta-rūpo'nanta-śrīr*
jitamanyur bhayāpahaḥ,
Caturasro gabhīrātmā
vidiśo vyādiśo diśaḥ.

Of infinite forms; of endless glories; who has conquered anger; dispeller of the fears of worldly life; who acts justly, giving a square deal to everyone; of unfathomable nature; distributor of fruits to persons according to their deserts; who issues commands to various cosmic forces; who reveals to the world by the scriptures the mystery of karma and its fruits.

101. *Anādir bhūrbhuvo lakṣmīḥ*
suvīro rūcirāṅgadaḥ,
Janano janajanmādir
bhīmo bhīma-parākramaḥ.

Who is the cause of all but has no other cause for Himself; support of the earth; beauty and splendor of the world; appearing in various lovely forms; wearing beautiful armlets; creator of all living creatures; root cause of the birth of all beings; terrifying to transgressors of His commands; striking His enemies with terror by His irresistible might.

102. *Ādhāranilayo dhātā*
puṣpahāsaḥ prajāgaraḥ,
Ūrdhvagaḥ satpathācāraḥ
prāṇadaḥ praṇavaḥ paṇaḥ.

Fundamental sustainer of all beings; requiring for Himself no support; blooming like a flower into the universe; ever awake and alert; on the top of everything; scrupulously walking on the path of truth and righteousness; life giver; Om; who first gave names for the things He created.

103. *Pramāṇaṁ prāṇanilayaḥ*
prāṇabhṛt prāṇajīvanaḥ,
Tattvaṁ tattvavid ekātmā
janma-mṛtyu-jarātigaḥ.

Proof of His own glory; root cause into which the vital airs go back at death; who takes the form of food and gives vitality to living beings; *prāna* of *prāna* (vital force); absolute reality; aware of the truth of Himself; sole, nondual Self of the universe; beyond birth, death, and age.

104. *Bhūr-bhuvaḥ-svas-tarus tāraḥ*
savitā prapitāmahaḥ,
Yajño yajñapatir yajvā
yajñāṅgo yajñavāhanaḥ.

Who created the tree of the three worlds by uttering the seed sounds *bhūh, bhuvah,* and *svah;* who helps to cross these worlds by these very sounds; father of all; father of the father of all beings; of the form of sacrifice; lord of sacrifices; performer of sacrifices; whose body consists of the things employed in a sacrifice; who ensures that sacrifices are conducted according to scriptural instructions.

105. *Yajñabhṛd yajñakṛd yajñī*
yajñabhug yajñasādhanaḥ,
Yajñāntakṛd yajñaguhyam
annam annāda eva ca.

Protector of sacrifices; performing sacrifices in the beginning and at the end of creation; the master to please whom all sacrifices are performed; enjoyer of sacrificial offerings; sacrifices to whom purify the mind, making it worthy of God-realization; giver of the reward of sacrifice; secret of sacrifice; Himself becoming food; eater of food.

106. *Ātmayoniḥ svayaṁjāto*
vaikhānaḥ sāmagāyanaḥ,
Devakīnandanaḥ sraṣṭā
kṣitīśaḥ pāpanāśanaḥ.

Material cause of creation; self-begotten; who, in the boar incarnation, dug through the earth deeper and deeper and killed Hiranyāksha, who lived in the nether regions; fond of singing the *Sāma Veda;* joy of mother Devakī; author of the whole world; who ruled the whole earth in the Rāma incarnation; who annihilates sins from men's hearts as they remember, worship, meditate on Him, and sing His praises and names.

107. *Śaṅkhabhṛn nandakī cakrī*
śārṅgadhanvā gadādharaḥ,
Rathāṅgapāṇir akṣobhyaḥ
sarva-praharaṇāyudhaḥ.

Sarva-praharaṇāyudha
om nama iti.

Bearer of the Pāñchajanya conch, which represents *prakriti*, from which the five elements arise; wearer of the Nandaka sword, which represents blissful knowledge; carrying the Sudarshana Chakra, which represents the mind; wielder of the Shārnga bow, which represents the ego; holder of the mace Kaumodakī, which represents the intellect; carrying the wheel of a chariot (the discus) in His hand; absolutely imperturbable; who employs everything as His most powerful weapon for destroying the mightiest enemies—supreme conqueror.

Thus, I bow to the supreme conqueror.

VIṢṆU SAHASRANĀMA MAHĀTMYAM

Glorification of the Thousand Names of Vishnu

1. *Itīdaṁ kīrtanīyasya*
   keśavasya mahātmanaḥ,
   Nāmnāṁ sahasraṁ divyānām
   aśeṣeṇa prakīrtitam.

In this manner, I have fully recited to you one thousand glorious names of Vishnu, of great-souled Keshava, who is worthy of being praised.

2. *Ya idaṁ śṛṇuyānnityaṁ*
   yaścāpi parikīrtayet,
   Nāśubhaṁ prāpnuyāt kiñcit
   so'mutreha ca mānavaḥ.

Whoever constantly hears this and who recites it as well, that man will not meet with any harm, either in this world or hereafter.

3. *Vedānta-go brāhmaṇaḥ syāt*
   kṣatriyo vijayī bhavet,
   Vaiśyo dhana-samṛddhaḥ syāc
   chūdraḥ sukham avāpnuyāt.

A Brāhmin will become expert in Vedānta; a Kshatriya (warrior) will be victorious; a Vaishya (businessman) will be blessed with wealth; and a Shūdra (menial worker) will obtain happiness.

4. *Dharmārthī prāpnuyād dharmam*
arthārthī cārtham āpnuyāt,
Kāmān avāpnuyāt kāmī
prajārthī cāpnuyāt prajām.

The seeker of righteousness will obtain righteousness; the seeker of wealth, wealth; the seeker of pleasure, pleasure; and the seeker of offspring, offspring.

5. *Bhaktimān yaḥ sadotthāya*
śucis tad-gata-mānasaḥ,
Sahasraṁ vāsudevasya
nāmnām etat prakīrtayet.

If, every day after getting up and purifying himself, a man of devotion fixes his mind on it and recites this (hymn) of Vāsudeva's thousand names,

6. *Yaśaḥ prāpnoti vipulaṁ*
jñāti-prādhānyam eva ca,
Acalāṁ śriyam āpnoti
śreyaḥ prāpnotyanuttamam.

He obtains immense fame and an exalted position in society; he obtains abiding glory; he attains the highest good, liberation.

7. *Na bhayaṁ kvacid āpnoti*
vīryaṁ tejaśca vindati,
Bhavatyarogo dyutimān
bala-rūpa-guṇānvitaḥ.

He has no fear anywhere; he acquires virility and radiance; he becomes free of disease; and he acquires glow and the qualities of strength and beauty.

8. *Rogārto mucyate rogād*
baddho mucyeta bandhanāt,
Bhayān mucyeta bhītas tu
mucyetāpanna āpadaḥ.

A man distressed by disease is freed from disease; the bound are freed from bondage; the fearful are freed from fear; the unfortunate are delivered from misfortunes.

9. *Durgāṇy-atitaraty-āśu*
puruṣaḥ puruṣottamam,
Stuvan nāma-sahasreṇa
nityaṁ bhakti-samanvitaḥ.

A man quickly crosses over all obstacles and sorrows by constantly praising with devotion the supreme person with the thousand names.

10. *Vāsudevāśrayo martyo*
vāsudeva-parāyaṇaḥ,
Sarva-pāpa-viśuddhātmā
yāti brahma sanātanam.

The soul of a mortal who has taken refuge in Vāsudeva (Krishna), having Vāsudeva as his supreme goal, is purified of sins and goes to the eternal absolute.

11. *Na vāsudeva-bhaktānāṁ*
aśubhaṁ vidyate kvacit,
Janma-mṛtyu-jarā-vyādhi-
bhayaṁ naivopajāyate.

Nowhere can harm befall the devotees of Vāsudeva; there is no fear of birth, death, old age, or disease for them.

12. *Imaṁ stavam adhīyānaḥ*
śraddhā-bhakti-samanvitaḥ,
Yujyetātmā sukha-kṣānti-
śrī-dhṛti-smṛti-kīrtibhiḥ.

By studying this hymn with faith and devotion, a man will obtain happiness of soul, patience, wealth, courage, memory, and fame.

13. *Na krodho na ca mātsaryaṁ*
na lobho nāśubhā matiḥ,
Bhavanti kṛta-puṇyānāṁ
bhaktānāṁ puruṣottame.

Neither anger nor pride nor greed nor an evil mind befalls those who have performed meritorious deeds, who are devoted to the supreme person.

14. *Dyauḥ sacandrārka-nakṣatrā*
khaṁ diśo bhūr mahodadhiḥ,
Vāsudevasya vīryeṇa
vidhṛtāni mahātmanaḥ.

The heavens together with the moon, sun, and constellations, the atmosphere, the directions, the earth, and the great ocean are supported by the power of the great soul, Vāsudeva.

15. *Sa-surāsura-gandharvaṁ*
sa-yakṣoraga-rākṣasam,
Jagadvaśe vartatedaṁ
kṛṣṇasya sa-carācaram.

Together with gods, devils, and celestial minstrels, fairies, snake spirits, and ogres, this world, both animate and inanimate, is under the control of Lord Krishna.

16. *Indriyāṇi mano buddhiḥ*
sattvaṁ tejo balaṁ dhṛtiḥ,
Vāsudevātmakāny-āhuḥ
kṣetraṁ kṣetrajña eva ca.

The sense organs, the mind, the intellect, the higher organ of intuition, radiance, strength, and endurance are only different forms of Vāsudeva; He is the field (objects of knowledge) as well as the knower of the field.

17. *Sarvāgamānām ācāraḥ*
prathamaṁ parikalpyate,
Ācāra-prabhavo dharmo
dharmasya prabhur acyutaḥ.

The teachings of all the scriptures emphasize righteous conduct. Without it, *dharma* has no meaning, and (the source of) righteousness is the infallible Lord.

18. *Ṛṣayaḥ pitaro devā*
mahā-bhūtāni dhātavaḥ,
Jaṅgamājaṅgamaṁ cedaṁ
jagan nārāyaṇodbhavam.

The *rishis,* ancestors, and gods, the great elements, all metals, and this world consisting of movable and immovable things have all sprung from God.

19. *Yogo jñānaṁ tathā sāṅkhyaṁ*
vidyāḥ śilpādi-karma ca,
Vedāḥ śāstrāṇi vijñānam
etat sarvaṁ janārdanāt.

The system of yoga, knowledge of the divine, also the Sānkhya philosophy, sciences, arts and crafts, the Vedas, the codes, and works of reflection emanate from Janārdana (one who brings men to their death).

20. *Eko viṣṇur mahad-bhūtaṁ*
pṛthag-bhūtāny-anekaśaḥ,
Trīṁllokān vyāpya bhūtātmā
bhuṅkte viśva-bhug avyayaḥ.

Vishnu, the great being, is one; individual beings are manifold. The immanent soul, the imperishable enjoyer of all, having pervaded the three worlds, experiences (pleasure and pain).

21. *Imaṁ stavaṁ bhagavato*
viṣṇor vyāsena kīrtitam,
Paṭhed ya icchet puruṣaḥ
śreyaḥ prāptuṁ sukhāni ca.

This eulogy of the blessed Vishnu, composed by Vyāsa, should be recited by a person who wishes to obtain happiness and the highest good.

22. *Viśveśvaram ajaṁ devaṁ*
jagataḥ prabhavāpyayam,
Bhajanti ye puṣkarākṣaṁ
na te yānti parā-bhavam.

Those who worship the lotus-eyed Lord of the universe, the unborn God, the creator and destroyer of the world, do not go to another birth.

Hariḥ om tat sat iti śrīman mahābhārate
Śatasāhasryāṁ saṁhitāyāṁ
Vaiyāsikyām ānuśāsanike parvaṇi
Dāna-dharmeṣu
Bhīṣma-yudhiṣṭhira-saṁvāde
Śrīviṣṇor divya-sahasra-nāma-stotram.

This noble act of reciting the *Vishnu Sahasranāma* is offered to Lord Hari.

(Thus ends) the sacred hymn of the Thousand Names of Vishnu, occurring in the dialogue on the themes of charity and righteousness between Bhīshma and Yudhishthira in the section entitled "Ānushāsanika" in the holy scripture *Mahābhārata,* which contains one hundred thousand verses.

Om pūrṇamadaḥ pūrṇamidaṁ
pūrṇāt pūrṇamudacyate,
Pūrṇasya pūrṇamādāya
pūrṇamevāvaśiṣyate.

Om śāntiḥ śāntiḥ śāntiḥ.

Om. That is perfect. This is perfect. From the perfect springs the perfect. If the perfect is taken from the perfect, the perfect remains.

Om. Peace! Peace! Peace!

ĀRATĪ

Morning and Evening Prayer

[Om] namaḥ pārvatī-pataye
Hara hara hara mahādev

Om! Salutations to Pārvatī's spouse. Hara, Hara, Hara, Mahādev!

Gaṇeśapurī yogabhūmī pavitra
Tithẽ nāndato yogirājā samartha
Tayā aṭhavītā̃ paramānanda prāpti
Namaskāra māzā śrī nityānandāsī

Ganeshpurī is the sacred land of yoga, where the worthy king of yogīs abides. By remembrance of him, supreme bliss is obtained. I bow to you, O venerable Nityānanda!

Āratī avadhūtā jaya jaya āratī gurunāthā

Refrain:
Āratī avadhūtā jaya jaya āratī gurunāthā

Wave lights to the Avadhūt. Glory! Glory! Wave lights to the lord of Gurus.

Jñāna-dāna deuni bhaktā (2x)
Sukha desī nityā
Jaya jaya āratī avadhūtā
(Refrain)

Imparting the gift of knowledge to your devotees, you give eternal happiness.

Mi-tũpaṇāce bhāva harapunī (2x)
Samatā de cittā
Jaya jaya āratī avadhūtā
(Refrain)

Taking away the sense of mine and yours, you give equal vision.

Nityānanda tũci datta (2x)
Harihara jagatrātā
Jaya jaya āratī avadhūtā
(Refrain)

O Nityānanda, you are truly Datta, Hari, and Hara, savior of the world.

Muktānanda mhaṇe śrīgurudevā (2x)
Tũci mātā-pitā
Jaya jaya āratī avadhūtā
(Refrain)

Muktānanda says, "O venerable Gurudeva, you are truly the mother and the father.

1. *Māgaṇẽ tẽ āhe eka tuzyā pāśī̃*
Deśīla tarī pāhī̃ śrīgurunāthā
Sarvadā vāce vado nityānanda nāma
Sarvā̃ bhūtī̃ maitrī āṇi muditā

Yā jagī̃ ghaḍo anavarata
viśva-bandhutva-prema
Cittapūrṇa sthiratā
Muktānanda mhaṇe śrīgurunāthā
Nāśa hoū̃ de yā jagācī viṣamatā

"There is a boon that I have to beg of you. Grant it, if you will, O venerable lord of Gurus! Let my voice always utter Nityānanda's name. Let all beings experience friendliness and joy. May brotherhood, love, and perfect steadiness of mind always prevail in the world!" Muktānanda implores, "O venerable lord of Gurus, let all inequality in the world be destroyed."

2. *Gajānanaṁ bhūta-gaṇādisevitaṁ*
Kapittha-jambū-phala-cāru-bhakṣaṇam
Umāsutaṁ śoka-vināśa-kārakaṁ
Namāmi vighneśvara-pāda-paṅkajam

Hariḥ om

O elephant-faced god, Ganesha, you are served by the assemblage of ghosts, and you eat sweet wood-apples and blackberries. You are Umā's son, the destroyer of sorrows. I bow to the lotus feet of the remover of obstacles. Hari Om.

3. *Om namaḥ śivāya gurave*
Sac-cid-ānanda-mūrtaye
Niṣprapañcāya śāntāya
Nirālambāya tejase

Om. Salutations to the Guru, who is Shiva! His form is being, consciousness, and bliss. He is transcendent, calm, free from all support, and luminous.

4. *Nityānandāya gurave*
Śiṣya-saṁsāra-hāriṇe
Bhakta-kāryaika-dehāya
Namaste cit-sad-ātmane

Salutations to Nityānanda, the Guru, who rescues his disciples from the cycle of birth and death, who has assumed a body to meet the needs of his devotees, and whose nature is consciousness and being.

5. *Vande devamumā-patiṁ suraguruṁ*
Vande jagat-kāraṇaṁ
Vande pannaga-bhūṣaṇaṁ mṛgadharaṁ
Vande paśūnāṁ patim

Vande sūrya-śaśāṅka-vahni-nayanaṁ
Vande mukunda-priyaṁ
Vande bhakta-janāśrayañca varadaṁ
Vande śivaṁ śaṅkaram

I adore the divine spouse of Umā. I adore the Guru of gods. I adore the cause of the universe. I adore the one who is embellished with snakes and who wears a deerskin. I adore the lord of bound creatures. I adore the one whose eyes are the sun, the moon, and fire. I adore the one who is dear to Mukunda (Vishnu). I adore the one who grants refuge to devotees and who is the giver of boons. I adore Shiva, who is Shankara, the benevolent.

6. *Śāntaṁ padmāsana-sthaṁ*
Śaśi-dhara-mukuṭaṁ pañca-vaktraṁ trinetraṁ
Śūlaṁ vajraṁ ca khaḍgaṁ
Paraśum abhayadaṁ dakṣiṇāṅge vahantam

Nāgaṁ pāśaṁ ca ghaṇṭāṁ
Ḍamaruka-sahitaṁ sāṅkuśaṁ vāma-bhāge
Nānā'laṅkāra-dīptaṁ
Sphaṭika-maṇi-nibhaṁ pārvatīśaṁ namāmi

The calm one is seated in the lotus posture with the moon as His crown. He has five faces and three eyes. With His five right hands He holds a trident, a thunderbolt, a sword, and an axe, and He makes the gesture granting fearlessness. His five left hands hold a snake, a noose, a bell, a tabor, and a goad. He is adorned with various ornaments and is pure and luminous like quartz. I bow to Pārvatī's lord.

7. *Karpūragauraṁ karuṇāvatāraṁ*
Saṁsāra-sāraṁ bhujagendra-hāram
Sadā vasantaṁ hṛdayāravinde
Bhavaṁ bhavānī-sahitaṁ namāmi

White as camphor, He is the incarnation of compassion, the essence of the universe, and He wears the lord of the serpents as a necklace. I bow to that Shiva who, with Pārvatī, always dwells in the lotus of the heart.

8. *Asita-giri-samaṁ syāt kajjalaṁ sindhu-pātre*
Sura-taru-vara-śākhā lekhanī patramurvī
Likhati yadi gṛhitvā śāradā sarvakālaṁ
Tadapi tava guṇānām īśa pāraṁ na yāti

Even if the black mountain were ink, the ocean an inkpot, a branch of the wish-fulfilling tree a pen, the earth a writing leaf and if, using all these, the goddess of learning were to write for eternity, the limit of Your virtues would not be reached.

9. *Tvameva mātā ca pitā tvameva*
Tvameva bandhuśca sakhā tvameva
Tvameva vidyā draviṇaṁ tvameva
Tvameva sarvaṁ mama deva deva

You are the mother, You are the father, You are the brother, You are the friend. You are knowledge, You are wealth. You are everything for me, O god of gods.

10. *Kara-caraṇa-kṛtaṁ vāk kāya-jaṁ karma-jaṁ vā*
Śravaṇa-nayana-jaṁ vā mānasaṁ vā'parādham
Vihitam-avihitaṁ vā sarvam etat kṣamasva
Jaya jaya karuṇābdhe śrīmahādeva śambho

Forgive all sins, whether committed by hands or feet, whether arising from speech, body, or actions, whether arising from ears, eyes, or mind. Forgive all actions of commission and omission. Glory! Glory! Ocean of mercy! O venerable great God Shiva!

11. *Candrodbhāsita-śekhare smara-hare*
Gaṅgā-dhare śaṅkare
Sarpair-bhūṣita-kaṇṭha-karṇa-vivare
Netrottha-vaiśvānare

Danti-tvak-kṛta-sundarāmbara-dhare
Trailokya-sāre hare

Mokṣārthaṁ kuru citta-vṛttim acalām
Anyaistu kiṁ karmabhiḥ

Shiva's forehead is illumined by the moon. He is the destroyer of the god of love, the bearer of the Gangā. His neck and ears are adorned with snakes. His third eye emits the Vaishvānara fire. He wears a garment of elephant skin. He is the essence of the three worlds. He is the remover of ignorance. Steady the flow of your thoughts to attain salvation. What is the use of other actions?

12. *Hariḥ om tatpuruṣāya vidmahe*
Mahādevāya dhīmahi
Tan-no rudraḥ pracodayāt

Hari Om. Let us know Shiva, the supreme being. Let us meditate on Shiva — Mahādeva. May that Shiva who is known as Rudra inspire us.

13. *Om namo'stvanantāya sahasra-mūrtaye*
Sahasra-pādā'kṣi-śiroru-bāhave
Sahasra-nāmne puruṣāya śāśvate
Sahasra-koṭī-yuga-dhāriṇe namaḥ

Salutations to the infinite Lord having infinite forms, infinite feet, eyes, heads, thighs, and arms. Salutations to the eternal being with infinite names who supports millions of cosmic ages.

14. *Viṣṇu-brahmendra-devai*
Rajata-giri-taṭāt prārthito yo'vatīrya
Śākyādy-uddāma-kaṇṭhī
Rava-nakhara-karā-ghāta-sañjāta-mūrcchām

Chando-dhenuṁ yatīndraḥ
Prakṛtim agamayat sūkti-pīyūṣa-varṣaiḥ
So'yaṁ śrīśaṅkarācaryo
Bhava-dava-dahanāt pātu lokān ajasram

Having been invoked by Vishnu, Brahmā, Indra, and other gods, Shiva descended from the lofty heights of the silver mountain, Kailāsa, and incarnated as Shankarāchārya, the king of ascetics. When the Vedic cow (the holy scriptures) had been struck unconscious by the shouts of the Buddhists and other nonbelievers, Shankarāchārya, the greatest of sages, revived her with the rains of his nectar-like words. May this venerable Shankarāchārya protect mankind forever from the burning fires of birth and death.

15. *Pūrṇaḥ pīyūṣa-bhānur*
Bhava-maru-tapanoddāma-tāpākulānāṁ
Prauḍhājñānāndhakārā-
Vṛta-viṣama-patha-bhrāmyatāmaṁśumālī;

Kalpaḥ śākhī yatīnāṁ
Vigata-dhana-sutādīṣaṇānāṁ sadā naḥ
Pāyācchrī-padma-pādā-
Dima-muni-sahitaḥ śrīmad-ācārya-varyaḥ

Shankarāchārya is the full moon showering his cooling nectar on those who are overwhelmed by the fierce heat of the sun in the desert of the world. He is the sun for those wandering on a rough road, wrapped in the thick folds of the darkness of ignorance. He is the wish-fulfilling tree for the ascetics who have overcome the desire for wealth, sons, and other things. May that venerable Shankarāchārya, the best of the Gurus, accompanied by his chief disciple, Padmapāda, protect us forever.

16. *Brahmānandaṁ paramasukhadaṁ*
Kevalaṁ jñāna-mūrtiṁ
Dvandvātītaṁ gagana-sadṛśaṁ
Tat-tvam-asy-ādi-lakṣyam

Ekaṁ nityaṁ vimalam acalaṁ
Sarvadhī-sākṣi-bhūtaṁ
Bhāvātītaṁ triguṇa-rahitaṁ
Sadguruṁ taṁ namāmi

He is absolute bliss, the bestower of supreme happiness, and he is the only one. He is the embodiment of knowledge, and he has transcended such dualities as pleasure and pain. He is all-pervasive, like the sky. He is the final goal of the Vedic dictum "Thou art That." He is one, eternal, pure, steadfast, and the witness of the intellects of all. He is beyond all states and devoid of the three *gunas: sattva, rajas,* and *tamas.* To him, to the Sadguru, I bow.

17. *Nārāyaṇaṁ padma-bhavaṁ vasiṣṭhaṁ*
Śaktiṁ ca tat-putra-parāśarañca
Vyāsaṁ śukaṁ gauḍa padaṁ mahāntaṁ
Govinda-yogīndram athāsya śiṣyam

Śrīśaṅkarācāryam athāsya padma-
Pādaṁ ca hastāmalakañca śiṣyam
Taṁ toṭakaṁ vārtika-kāram anyān
Asmad-gurūn santatam ānato'smi

To Nārāyana; to the lotus-born Brahmā; to Vasishtha; to Shakti and to Shakti's son Parāshara; to Vyāsa; to Shuka; to the great Gaudapāda; to Govindapāda, greatest of yogīs; to his disciple Shankarāchārya; to his disciples, Padmapāda, Hastāmalaka, Totakāchārya, and Sureshvarāchārya, writer of the commentary; and to the other Gurus of our lineage, I bow forever.

18. *Viśvaṁ darpaṇa-dṛśyamāna-nagarī-*
Tulyaṁ nijāntargataṁ
Paśyannātmani māyayā bahir-ivod-
Bhūtaṁ yathā nidrayā

Yaḥ sākṣāt kurute prabodha-samaye
Svātmānam evādvayaṁ
Tasmai śrīguru-mūrtaye nama idaṁ
Śrīdakṣiṇā-mūrtaye

I bow to the Guru, Shrī Dakshināmūrti, who looks upon the universe as being within himself but appearing, by the power of *māyā,* to be outside, like a city reflected in a mirror or a dream in sleep. By the awakening of the real knowledge he realizes that there is nothing else except his own Self.

19. *Akhaṇḍa-maṇḍalākāraṁ*
Vyāptaṁ yena carācaram
Tat-padaṁ darśitam yena
Tasmai śrīgurave namaḥ

Salutations to the Guru, who reveals that Reality which pervades the spherical universe composed of the sentient and insentient.

20. *Gururbrahmā gururviṣṇur*
Gururdevo maheśvaraḥ
Guruḥ sākṣāt paraṁ brahma
Tasmai śrīgurave namaḥ

Salutations to the Guru, who is Brahmā, the creator; Vishnu, the sustainer; Shiva, the destroyer; and the manifestation of the supreme absolute.

21. *Śruti-smṛti-purāṇānām*
Ālayaṁ karuṇālayam
Namāmi bhagavat-pādaṁ
Śaṅkaraṁ loka-śaṅkaram

I bow to the feet of the glorious Shankarāchārya, who is the abode of the Vedas (revealed scriptures), Smritis (laws of discipline), and Purānas (religious myths) and who is the abode of compassion, the incarnation of Shiva, and the benefactor of the world.

22. *Śaṅkaraṁ śaṅkarācāryaṁ*
Keśavaṁ bādarāyaṇam
Sūtra-bhāṣya-kṛtau vande
Bhagavantau punaḥ punaḥ

I bow again and again to Shankarāchārya, the incarnation of Shankara, and to Bādarāyana (Vyāsa), the incarnation of Vishnu, who are, respectively, the commentator and the author of the *Brahma Sūtras.*

23. *Īśvaro gurur-ātmeti*
Mūrti-bheda-vibhāgine
Vyomavad vyāpta-dehāya
Dakṣiṇā-mūrtaye namaḥ

Although He has assumed the threefold role of the Lord, the Guru, and the Self, His body is all-pervasive like space. I bow to that Dakshināmūrti.

24. *Hariḥ om yajñena yajñam ayajanta devā-*
Stāni dharmāṇi prathamānyāsan
Te ha nākaṁ mahimānaḥ
Sacanta yatra pūrve sādhyāḥ santi devāḥ

Hari Om. Godlike men performed sacrifices in the form of good deeds, which were accepted as the first religious duties. Through the merit of these deeds they attained heaven, where the Sādhya deities and gods dwell.

25. *Om rājādhirājāya prasahya-sāhine*
Namo vayaṁ vaiśravaṇāya kurmahe
Sa me kāmān kāma-kāmāya mahyaṁ
Kāmeśvaro vaiśravaṇo dadātu
Kuberāya vaiśravaṇāya mahārājāya namaḥ

Om. Let us bow to Kubera, the king of kings, who gives without motive. Let Kubera, the lord of desires, grant me, who desires everything, the objects of my desires. Salutations to Kubera, the great king, the son of Vishravana.

26. *Om viśvataś-cakṣuruta viśvato-mukho*
Viśvato-bāhuruta viśvatas-pāt
Sambāhubhyāṁ dhamati sam-pa[ta]trair
Dyāvā-bhūmī janayan deva ekaḥ

Om. He has eyes and mouths on all sides. His arms and feet are everywhere. He gives arms to men and wings to birds. He is the one Lord, who creates both heaven and earth.

27. *Nānā-sugandha-puṣpāṇi*
Yathā-kālodbhavāni ca
Puṣpāñjaliṁ mayā dattaṁ
Gṛhāṇa parameśvara

With cupped hands, I offer flowers of various scents blooming in this season. Accept them, O Parameshvara, O supreme God.

28. *Ityeṣā vāṅmayī pūjā*
Śrīmacchaṅkara-pādayoḥ
Arpitā tena deveśaḥ
Prīyatāṁ me sadāśivaḥ

This is the hymnal worship that I offer at the feet of Lord Shankara. By its merits, may the lord of gods, the ever-beneficent Shiva, be pleased with me.

29. *Yad akṣaraṁ padaṁ bhraṣṭaṁ*
Mātrā-hīnaṁ ca yad bhavet
Tat-sarvaṁ kṣamyatāṁ deva
Prasīda parameśvara

If a letter or a word has been left out, or if any letter is mispronounced, please forgive me, O God, and be gracious.

30. *Om pūrṇamadaḥ pūrṇamidaṁ*
Pūrṇāt pūrṇamudacyate
Pūrṇasya pūrṇamādāya
Pūrṇamevāvaśiṣyate

Om. That is perfect. This is perfect. From the perfect springs the perfect. If the perfect is taken from the perfect, the perfect remains.

Om śāntiḥ śāntiḥ śāntiḥ
Om. Peace! Peace! Peace!

Hare Rām Hare Rām
Rām Rām Hare Hare
Hare Kṛṣṇa Hare Kṛṣṇa
Kṛṣṇa Kṛṣṇa Hare Hare (5x)

Hariḥ om tat-sat (3x)
Sadgurunāth Mahārāj kī Jay

Om tat-sat is recited to dedicate an action to God. *Om* is the primal sound and thus the first name of God—the first manifestation of consciousness. *Tat* implies that everything belongs to Him. *Sat* refers to good deeds and duties well performed.

Sadgurunāth Mahārāj kī Jay is a salutation of joy and reverence that means "Hail the true Guru," who is the Self of all.

Upanishad Mantras

1. *Agnir yathaiko bhuvanaṁ praviṣṭo*
Rūpaṁ rūpaṁ pratirūpo babhūva
Ekas tathā sarva-bhūtāntarātmā
Rūpaṁ rūpaṁ pratirūpo bahiśca

There is one fire that enters the world and assumes the forms of the objects it enters; likewise, the one inner Self of all beings assumes the forms of whatever it enters, while continuing to exist outside all forms.

2. *Vāyur yathaiko bhuvanaṁ praviṣṭo*
Rūpaṁ rūpaṁ pratirūpo babhūva
Ekas tathā sarva-bhūtāntarātmā
Rūpaṁ rūpaṁ pratirūpo bahiśca

There is one air that enters the world and assumes the forms of the objects it enters; likewise, the one inner Self of all beings assumes the forms of whatever it enters, while continuing to exist outside all forms.

3. *Sūryo yathā sarva-lokasya cakṣur*
Na lipyate cākṣuṣair bāhya-doṣaiḥ
Ekas tathā sarva-bhūtāntarātmā
Na lipyate loka-duḥkhena bāhyaḥ

The sun, which is the eye of the whole world, is not affected by the impurities of the eyes of the common people, which are external to it; likewise, the one inner Self of all beings is not affected by the sorrows of the world, which are external to it.

4. *Eko vaśī sarva-bhūtāntarātmā*
Ekaṁ rūpaṁ bahudhā yaḥ karoti
Taṁ ātma-sthaṁ ye'nupaśyanti dhīrās
Teṣāṁ sukhaṁ śāśvataṁ netareṣām

He is the controlling one, the inner Self of all beings, who makes His one form manifold. Only those steadfast ones who realize Him as seated in the Self experience eternal bliss. This bliss does not belong to anyone else.

5. *Nityo'nityānāṁ cetanaś cetanānāṁ*
Eko bahūnāṁ yo vidadhāti kāmān
Taṁ ātma-sthaṁ ye'nupaśyanti dhīrās
Teṣāṁ śāntiḥ śāśvatī netareṣām

The Self is eternal amid the transient; pure consciousness amid limited consciousness; one among many; and the fulfiller of all desires. Only those steadfast ones who realize Him as seated in the Self experience eternal peace. This peace does not belong to anyone else.

Śuka uvāca:

6. *Mahā-prasāde govinde*
Nāmni brahmaṇi vaiṣṇave
Svalpa-puṇyavatāṁ rājan
Viśvāso naiva jāyate

Shuka said:

O king, those who have little merit do not have faith in divine grace, Lord Govinda, holy names, Brāhmins, or Vaishnavas.

7. *Yaṁ śaivāḥ samupāsate śiva iti*
Brahmeti vedāntino
Bauddhā buddha iti pramāṇa-paṭavaḥ
Karteti naiyāyikāḥ

Arhannity-atha jaina-śāsana-ratāḥ
Karmeti mīmāṁsakāḥ
So'yaṁ vo vidadhātu vāñchita-phalaṁ
Trailokya-nātho hariḥ

The Lord is adored by the Shaivites as Shiva; by the Vedāntins as Brahman; by the Buddhists as Buddha; by the logicians, skilled in reasoning, as the Creator; by the Jains as the Arhat; and by the ritualists as Sacrifice. Let that Hari, the lord of the three worlds, grant you the desired fruit.

8. *Na deśa-niyamo rājan*
Na kāla-niyamas tathā
Vidyate nātra sandeho
Viṣṇu-nāmānukīrtane

O king, there is no doubt that there are no limitations of place or time for chanting the names of Vishnu.

9. *Kālo'sti yajña-dāne vā*
Snāne kālo'sti vā jape
Viṣṇu-saṅkīrtane kālo
Nāstyatra pṛthivīpate

An auspicious hour is required for a sacrifice, a charitable gift, a bath, or *japa,* but, O lord of the earth, there is no restriction of time for chanting the names of Vishnu.

10. *Nikaṭam eva ḍṛśyate*
Kṛtānta-nagaraṁ dhruvam
Śivaṁ smara śivaṁ dhyāhi
Śivaṁ cintaya sarvadā

The unchanging city of death is indeed approaching quite near; therefore, always remember Shiva, meditate on Shiva, and contemplate Shiva.

11. *Ahaṁ śivaḥ śivaścāyaṁ*
Tvaṁ cāpi śiva eva hi
Sarvaṁ śivamayaṁ brahma
Śivāt paraṁ na kiñcana

I am Shiva, this is Shiva, and indeed you, too, are nothing but Shiva. The entire cosmos is an embodiment of the Absolute. There is nothing higher than Shiva.

12. *Sūkṣmātisūkṣmaṁ kalilasya madhye*
Viśvasya sraṣṭāram aneka-rūpam
Viśvasyaikaṁ pariveṣṭitāraṁ
Jñātvā śivaṁ śāntim atyantam eti

He will attain infinite peace who knows that Shiva resides in the hearts of all, that He is the subtlest of the subtle, the creator of the universe, the many-formed, and the one who envelops the cosmos.

13. *Sarvagaṁ sarvakartāraṁ*
Sarvaṁ sarvāvabhāsakam
Sarvāvalambanaṁ śāntaṁ
Śivaṁ purṇaṁ bhajāmyaham

I adore the peaceful, benevolent, and perfect One, who is all-pervasive, who is the doer of all, who is all, who is the illuminator of all, and who is the support of all.

14. *Sargādi-kāle bhagavān virañcir*
Upāsyainaṁ sarga-sāmarthyamāpa
Tutoṣa citte vāñchitārthāṁśca labdhvā
Dhanyaḥ sopāsyopāsako bhavati dhātā

Before starting the creation, Lord Brahmā, having worshipped Shiva, obtained the power of creation. Having obtained his desired objective, he was satisfied at heart. Blessed is Brahmā, who, being worthy of worship, becomes the worshipper of Shiva.

15. *Kulaṁ pavitraṁ pitaraḥ samuddhṛtā*
Vasundharā tena ca pāvitā dvijāḥ
Sanātano'nādir ananta-vigraho
Hṛdi sthito yasya sadaiva śaṅkaraḥ

Shankara is primal, beginningless, and assumes infinite forms. The family of a person in whose heart Shankara is forever established is holy. His ancestors are elevated, and the earth and Brāhmins are purified."

Śibiruvāca:

16. *Sarve'tra sukhinaḥ santu*
Sarve santu nirāmayāḥ
Sarve bhadrāṇi paśyantu
Mā kaścid duḥkham āpnuyāt

King Shibi said:
Let people everywhere be happy. Let everyone be free of disease. Let everyone see good everywhere. Let no one meet with sorrow.

Om śāntiḥ śāntiḥ śāntiḥ Om. Peace! Peace! Peace!

ŚIVA MAHIMNAḤ STOTRAM

Hymn to the Glory of Shiva

[Om namaḥ] pārvatī-pataye
Hara hara hara mahādev.

Om! Salutations to Pārvatī's consort. Hara, Hara, Hara, Mahādev!

Gajānanaṁ bhūta-gaṇādi-sevitaṁ
Kapittha-jambū-phalacāru-bhakṣaṇam,
Umāsutaṁ śoka-vināśa-kārakaṁ
Namāmi vighne-śvara-pāda-paṅkajam.

O elephant-faced god, Ganesha, you are served by the assemblage of ghosts, and you eat sweet wood-apples and blackberries. You are Umā's son, the destroyer of sorrows. I bow to the lotus feet of the remover of obstacles.

Śrī-puṣpadanta uvāca:

1. *Mahimnaḥ pāraṁ te*
parama-viduṣo yadya-sadṛśī,
Stutir-brahmā-dīnām-
api tadava-sannā-stvayi giraḥ;
Athā-vācyaḥ sarvaḥ
svamati-pariṇā-māvadhi gṛṇan,
Mamā-pyeṣaḥ stotre
hara nir-apavādaḥ parikaraḥ.

Shrī Pushpadanta said:

If it is unseemly to praise You when ignorant of the extent of Your greatness, then even the praises of Brahmā and others are inadequate. If no blame is attached to those who praise You according to their intellectual capacity, then even I should not be reproached for my attempt to compose this hymn.

2. *Atītaḥ panthānaṁ*
tava ca mahimā vāṅmanasayor-
Atad-vyā-vṛttyā yaṁ
cakita-mabhi-dhatte śruti-rapi;
Sa kasya stotavyaḥ
kati-vidha-guṇaḥ kasya viṣayaḥ,
Pade tvar-vācīne
patati na manaḥ kasya na vacaḥ.

Your greatness is beyond the reach of mind and speech. Who can properly praise that which even the Vedas describe with trepidation as "not this, not this"? How many qualities do You possess? By whom can You be perceived? And yet whose mind and speech do not turn to the form You later assume?

3. *Madhu-sphītā-vācaḥ*
parama-mamṛtaṁ nirmi-tavatas,
Tava brahman kiṁ vāg-
api sura-guror-vismaya-padam;
Mama tvetāṁ vāṇīṁ
guṇa-kathana-puṇyena-bha-vataḥ,
Punāmītyarthe'smin
puramathana buddhir-vya-vasitā.

O Brahman, is it any wonder that Brihaspati, the preceptor of gods, praises You, who are the author of the nectarean Vedas? O destroyer of Tripura, the three cities of the three sons of the demon Tāraka, the thought that by praising Your glories I shall purify my speech has prompted me to undertake this work.

4. *Tavaiś-varyaṁ yat-taj-*
jaga-dudaya-rakṣā-pralaya-kṛt,
Trayī-vastu vyastaṁ
tisṛṣu guṇa-bhinnāsu tanuṣu;
Abha-vyānā-masmin
varada ramaṇī-yāma-ramaṇīm,
Vihantuṁ vyā-krośīṁ
vida-dhata ihaike jaḍa-dhiyaḥ.

O giver of boons, some thick-headed people, in order to refute Your divinity, invent arguments that are pleasing to the ignorant but are in fact hateful. You are described by the three Vedas as Brahmā the creator, Vishnu the sustainer, and Shiva the destroyer of the world according to the corresponding qualities of the three *gunas.*

5. *Kimīhaḥ kiṁkayaḥ*
sa khalu kimupāya-stri-bhuvanam,
Kimā-dhāro dhātā
sṛjati kimu-pādāna iti ca;
Atar-kyaiś-varye tvay-
yana-vasara-duḥstho hatadhiyaḥ,
Kutarko'yaṁ kāṁścin
mukha-rayati mohāya jagataḥ.

Fulfilling what desire, assuming what form, and using what instruments, support, and material does the creator make the three worlds? This kind of futile argumentation about You, whose divine nature is beyond the reach of intellect, makes the deluded vociferous and deceives men.

6. *Ajanmāno lokāḥ*
   kima-vayava-vanto'pi jagatām-
   Adhiṣṭhā-tāraṁ kiṁ
   bhava-vidhi-ranāḍṛtya bhavati;
   Anīśo vā kuryād-
   bhuvana-janane kaḥ parikaro,
   Yato mandās-tvāṁ prat-
   yama-ravara saṁśerata ime.

O lord of gods, can the worlds be without origin although they have parts? Is their creation possible without a creator? Who else but God can initiate the creation of the worlds? Because they are fools they raise such doubts about Your existence.

7. *Trayī sāṅkhyaṁ yogaḥ*
   paśu-pati-mataṁ vaiṣṇava-miti,
   Prabhinne prasthāne
   para-mida-madaḥ pathya-miti ca;
   Rucīnāṁ vaici-tryād-
   ṛju-kuṭila-nānā-patha-juṣām,
   Nṛṇā-meko gamyas-
   tvamasi payasā-marṇava iva.

Different paths to realization are prescribed by the three Vedas, by the Sānkhya, Yoga, and Shaiva doctrines, and by the Vaishnava *shāstras.* People follow different paths, straight or crooked, considering one best or most appropriate for their temperament, but all paths lead to You, just as different rivers flow into the same ocean.

8. *Mahokṣaḥ khaṭ-vāṅgaṁ*
paraśu-rajinaṁ bhasma phaṇinaḥ,
Kapālaṁ cetīyat-
tava varada tantro-pakaraṇam;
Surās-tāṁ taṁ-ṛddhiṁ
dadhati tu bhavad-bhrū-praṇi-hitāṁ,
Na hi svātma-rāmaṁ
viṣaya-mṛga-tṛṣṇā bhramayati.

O giver of boons, a great bull, a wooden club, an axe, a tiger skin, ashes, serpents, a human skull, and other such things—these are Your sole possessions, although simply by casting Your glance You gave the gods great treasures, which they enjoy. Truly, the mirage of sense objects cannot delude one whose delight is in the Self.

9. *Dhruvaṁ kaś-cit sarvaṁ*
sakala-mapara-stva-dhruva-midam,
Paro dhrau-vyā-dhrauvye
jagati gadati vyasta-viṣaye;
Samaste'pye-tasmin
pura-mathana tair-vismita iva,
Stuvañ-jihremi tvāṁ
na khalu nanu dhṛṣṭā mukharatā.

O destroyer of the demon Pura, some say the whole universe is eternal, whereas others say it is ephemeral. Still others contend that it is both eternal and noneternal, having different characteristics. Bewildered by all this, I do not feel ashamed to praise You; indeed, my verbosity indicates my audacity.

10. *Tavaiś-varyaṁ yatnād-*
yadupari viriñcir-hari-radhaḥ,

Paricchettuṁ yātāv
anala-manala-skandha-vapuṣaḥ;
Tato bhakti-śraddhā
bhara-guru-gṛṇad-bhyāṁ giriśa yat,
Svayaṁ tasthe tābhyāṁ
tava kimanu-vṛttirna phalati.

O Girisha, when You took the form of a pillar of fire, neither Brahmā trying from above nor Vishnu trying from below was able to measure You. Afterward, when they praised You with great faith and devotion, You revealed Yourself to them of Your own accord, thus indicating that worshipping You does indeed bear fruit.

11. *Ayatnā-dāpādya*
tribhuvana-mavaira-vyati-karam,
Daśāsyo yad-bāhūn-
abhṛta raṇa-kaṇḍū-para-vaśān;
Śiraḥ-padma-śreṇī-
racita-caraṇām-bhoru-habaleḥ,
Sthirāyās-tvad-bhaktes
tripura-hara visphūr-jitamidam.

O destroyer of Tripura, it was because of his great devotion that the ten-headed Rāvana still had arms and was eager for fresh war after he had easily rid the three worlds of all traces of enemies. That same devotion prompted him to offer his heads as lotuses to Your feet.

12. *Amuṣya tvatsevā-*
samadhi-gata-sāraṁ bhuja-vanam,
Balāt-kailāse'pi
tvadadhi-vasatau vikrama-yataḥ;

Alabhyā pātāle
'pyalasa-cali-tāṅ-guṣṭha-śirasi,
Pratiṣṭhā tvay-yāsīd
dhruva-mupacito muhyati khalaḥ.

But when Rāvana, whose strength was obtained by worshipping You, attempted to possess Kailāsa, Your abode, with the valor of his arms, You moved the tip of Your toe, and he did not find a resting place even in the nether world. Truly, when affluent, the wicked become deluded.

13. *Yadṛddhiṁ sutrāmṇo*
varada paramo-ccairapi satīm-
Adhaś-cakre bāṇaḥ
pari-jana-vidheya-tri-bhuvanaḥ;
Na taccitraṁ tasmin-
vari-vasitari tvaccaraṇayor,
Na kasyā unnatyai
bhavati śirasas-tvay-yavanatiḥ.

O giver of boons, it is no wonder that Bāna, the Asura king who worshipped Your feet, had the three worlds at his command and shamed the wealth of Indra. What prosperity does not result from bowing one's head to You!

14. *Akāṇḍa-brahmāṇḍa-*
kṣaya-cakita-devā-sura-kṛpā,
Vidheya-syā-sīdyas-
trina-yana viṣaṁ saṁ-hṛta-vataḥ;
Sa kalmāṣaḥ kaṇṭhe
tava na kurute na śriya-maho,
Vikāro'pi ślāghyo
bhuvana-bhaya-bhaṅga-vyasaninaḥ.

O three-eyed one, You drank poison out of compassion for gods and demons when they were distraught over the threatened destruction of the universe, but surely the dark blue stain it left on Your throat only enhanced Your beauty.

15. *Asid-dhārthā naiva*
kvacidapi sadevā-suranare,
Nivar-tante nityaṁ
jagati jayino yasya viśi-khāḥ;
Sa paś-yannīśa tvāṁ
itara-surasā-dhāraṇa-mabhūt,
Smaraḥ smarta-vyātmā
na hi vaśiṣu pathyaḥ pari-bhavaḥ.

O Lord, the god of love, Kāma, whose arrows never fail in the world of gods, demons, or men, became simply an object of memory because he regarded You as an ordinary god. An insult to the self-controlled is not conducive to well-being.

16. *Mahī pādā-ghā-tād*
vrajati sahasā saṁ-śaya-padam,
Padaṁ viṣṇor-bhrām-yad
bhuja-parigha-rugṇa-graha-gaṇam;
Muhur-dyaur-dauḥsthyaṁ yāt-
yani-bhṛta-jaṭā-tāḍita-taṭā,
Jagad-rakṣāyai tvaṁ
naṭasi nanu vāmaiva vibhutā.

When You danced to save the world, the earth, at the striking of Your feet, wondered whether it would not come to sudden destruction, as did the spatial regions and the multitude of planets, being oppressed by the movement of Your iron, club-like arms; and heaven became miserable as its side was constantly struck by Your waving, matted hair. Ah, Your very mightiness was the cause of the trouble.

17. *Viyad-vyāpī tārā-*
    gaṇa-guṇita-phenod-gama-ruciḥ,
Pravāho vārāṁ yaḥ
    pṛṣata-laghu-dṛṣṭaḥ śirasi te;
Jagad-dvīpā-kāraṁ
    jaladhi-valayaṁ tena kṛtami-
Tyanenai-vonne-yaṁ
    dhṛta-mahima divyaṁ tava vapuḥ.

The Mandākinī River, which pervades the sky and whose crests of foam become more beautiful because of the stars and planets within it, seems no more than a drop of water when on Your head. That same river has turned the world into seven islands surrounded by waters. From this can be inferred the vastness of Your divine body.

18. *Rathaḥ kṣoṇī yantā*
    śata-dhṛti-ragendro dhanu-ratho,
Rathāṅge candrār-kau
    ratha-caraṇa-pāṇiḥ śara iti;
Didha-kṣoste ko'yaṁ
    tripura-tṛṇa-māḍam-bara-vidhir,
Vidheyaiḥ krīḍantyo
    na khalu para-tantrāḥ prabhu-dhiyaḥ.

When You wanted to burn the three cities, which were but a piece of straw to You, the earth was Your chariot; Brahmā, Your charioteer; the great mountain Meru, Your bow; the sun and the moon, the wheels of Your chariot; and Vishnu, Your arrow. Why all this paraphernalia? The Lord is not dependent on others. He was only playing with the objects at His command.

19. *Hariste sāhasraṁ*
kamala-balimā-dhāya padayor,
Yade-kone tasmin-
nija-muda-haran-netra-kamalam;
Gato bhaktyu-drekaḥ
pariṇati-masau cakra-vapuṣā,
Trayāṇāṁ rakṣāyai
tripura-hara jāgarti jagatām.

O destroyer of Tripura, Hari rooted out his own lotus eye to replace a single flower that was missing from his offering of a thousand lotuses to Your feet. His exuberance of devotion was transformed into the Sudarshana Chakra, the discus that remains alert to protect the three worlds.

20. *Kratau supte jāgrat-*
tvamasi phala-yoge kratu-matām,
Kva karma pradh-vastaṁ
phalati puruṣā-rādhana-mṛte;
Atas-tvāṁ saṁ-prekṣya
kratuṣu phala-dāna-prati-bhuvaṁ,
Śrutau śraddhāṁ baddhvā
dṛḍha-parikaraḥ karmasu janaḥ.

When a sacrifice is ended, You remain awake to bestow its fruit on the sacrificer. How can any action bear fruit if not accompanied by worship of You, O Lord? Therefore, knowing You to be the giver of fruits of sacrifices and putting faith in the Vedas, people become steadfast in the performance of sacrificial acts.

21. *Kriyā-dakṣo dakṣaḥ*
kratupati-radhīśa-stanu-bhṛtām-
Ṛṣīṇā-mārtvijyaṁ
śaraṇada sadasyāḥ suragaṇāḥ;
Kratu-bhraṁśas-tvattaḥ
kratu-phala-vidhāna-vyasanino,
Dhruvaṁ kartuḥ śraddhā
vidhura-mabhi-cārāya hi makhāḥ.

O giver of refuge, You, who are always intent on awarding the fruits of sacrifices, destroyed even that sacrifice in which Daksha, the lord of creation and an expert in sacrificial rites, was the sacrificer, *rishis* were priests, and gods were supervisors. Surely sacrifices cause injury to the sacrificers in the absence of devotion.

22. *Prajā-nāthaṁ nātha*
prasabha-mabhikaṁ svāṁ duhitaram,
Gataṁ rohid-bhūtāṁ
rira-mayiṣu-mṛṣyasya vapuṣā;
Dhanuṣ-pāṇer-yātaṁ
divamapi sapatrā-kṛtamamum,
Trasantaṁ te'dyāpi
tyajati na mṛga-vyādha-rabhasaḥ.

O Lord, when Brahmā was overcome by incestuous lust, his daughter transformed herself into a hind to get away, but he became a stag in order to ravish her. Although keenly pierced by Your arrows, Brahmā fled fearfully to the sky, and even now Your fury as a hunter with bow in hand does not leave him.

23. *Sva-lāvaṇyā-śaṁsā*
dhṛta-dhanuṣa-mahnāya tṛṇavat-
Puraḥ pluṣṭaṁ dṛṣṭvā
pura-mathana puspā-yudhamapi;
Yadi straiṇaṁ devī
yama-nirata dehārdha-ghatanā-
Davaiti tvāmaddhā
bata varada mugdhā yuvatayaḥ.

O destroyer of Tripura, O giver of boons, Pārvatī saw the god of love with bow in hand burned by You in a moment like a piece of straw. O You who are engaged in austerities, if she, who is proud of her beauty, believes that You are fascinated by her because she occupies half of Your body, let her. Young women are simple-minded.

24. *Śma-śāne-ṣvā-krīḍā*
smara-hara piśā-cāḥ saha-carāś,
Citā-bhasmā-lepaḥ
sragapi nṛkaroṭī-parikaraḥ;
Amāṅ-galyaṁ śīlaṁ
tava bhavatu nāmaiva-makhilam,
Tathāpi smar-tṝṇāṁ
varada paramaṁ maṅ-galamasi.

O destroyer of the god of love, O giver of boons, Your play is in cremation grounds, Your companions are ghosts, You smear Your body with the ashes of burned bodies and wear human skulls as Your garlands — all Your conduct is truly inauspicious. But You promote the greatest good for those who remember You.

25. *Manaḥ prat-yak-citte*
savidha-mava-dhāyātta-marutaḥ,
Prahṛṣyad-romāṇaḥ
pramada-salilot-saṅgita-dṛśaḥ;
Yadā-lokyāh-lādaṁ
hrada iva nimaj-jyā-mṛtamaye,
Dadhatyantas-tattvaṁ
kimapi yaminas-tat kila bhavān.

You are indeed that unspeakable truth which yogīs realize through meditating on the Self and controlling the breath according to the directions laid down in the scriptures. Realizing this truth, they experience thrills of ecstasy and their eyes brim with tears of joy; swimming in a pool of nectar, they enjoy inner bliss.

26. *Tvamarka-stvaṁ somas-*
tvamasi pavanas-tvam huta-vahas-
Tvamāpas-tvaṁ vyoma
tvamu-dharaṇi-rātmā tvamiti ca;
Paricchin-nām-evaṁ
tvayi pari-ṇatā bibhratu giraṁ,
Na vidma-stat-tattvaṁ
vaya-miha tu yat-tvam na bhavasi.

The wise hold this limiting view of You: You are the sun, You are the moon, You are fire, You are air, You are water, You are space, You are the earth, and You are the Self. But we do not know that thing which You are not.

27. *Trayīṁ tisro vṛttīs-*
tribhuvana-matho trīnapi surā-
Nakārā-dyair-varṇais-
tribhi-rabhi-dadhat-tīrṇa-vikṛti;

Turīyaṁ te dhāma
dhvani-bhirava-rundhāna-maṇubhiḥ,
Samastaṁ vyastaṁ tvāṁ
śaraṇada gṛṇātyomiti padam.

O giver of refuge, when considered separately, the three letters of the word *Aum (Om)*—*a, u, m*—indicate the three Vedas, the three states, the three worlds, and the three gods and thus describe You as being diverse. But united by its subtle sound, the word *Om* denotes You in Your absolute transcendental state.

28. *Bhavaḥ śarvo rudraḥ*
paśupati-rathograḥ saha-mahāṁ-
Stathā bhīmeśānā-
viti yadabhi-dhānāṣṭakam-idam;
Amuṣmin-pratyekaṁ
pravi-carati deva śruti-rapi,
Priyāyāsmai dhāmne
pravihi-tanamasyo'smi bhavate.

O Lord! Bhava, Sharva, Rudra, Pashupati, Ugra, Mahādeva, Bhīma, and Īshāna—these eight names of Yours are each treated in detail in the Vedas. To You, most beloved Lord Shankara of resplendent form, I offer salutations.

29. *Namo nediṣṭhāya*
priya-dava davi-ṣṭhāya ca namo,
Namaḥ kṣodiṣṭhāya
smarahara mahiṣṭhāya ca namaḥ;
Namo varṣiṣṭhāya
trinayana yaviṣṭhāya ca namo,
Namaḥ sarvasmai te
tadida-mati-sarvāya ca namaḥ.

O lover of fire, my salutations to You, who are the nearest and the farthest. O destroyer of the god of love, my salutations to You, who are the minutest and the largest. O three-eyed one, my salutations again and again to You, who are all and beyond all.

30. *Bahala-rajase viśvot-pattau*
bhavāya namo namaḥ,
Prabala-tamase tat-saṁhāre
harāya namo namaḥ;
Jana-sukhakṛte sattvo-driktau
mṛḍāya namo namaḥ,
Prama-hasi pade nistrai-guṇye
śivāya namo namaḥ.

Salutations to You as Brahmā, in whom *rajas* predominates for the creation of the universe; salutations to You as Rudra, in whom *tamas* predominates for its destruction; and salutations to You as Vishnu, in whom *sattva* predominates for its preservation. Salutations to You, O Shiva, who are effulgent and beyond the three *gunas.*

31. *Kṛśa-pari-ṇati cetaḥ kleśa-vaśyaṁ kva cedaṁ*
Kva-ca tava guṇa-sīmol-laṅ-ghinī
śaśva-dṛddhiḥ,
Iti cakita-mamandī-kṛtya māṁ bhakti-rādhād
Varada caraṇa-yo-ste vākya-puṣpo-pahāram.

O giver of boons, how poor is my ill-developed mind, subject to misery, and how boundless is Your divinity, eternal and possessing infinite virtues. Although terror stricken because of this, I am inspired by my devotion to offer this hymnal garland at Your feet.

32. *Asita-giri-samaṁ syāt-kajjalaṁ sindhu-pātre*
Sura-taru-vara-śākhā lekhanī patra-murvī,
Likhati yadi gṛhītvā śāradā sarva-kālaṁ
Tadapi tava guṇānāmīśa pāraṁ na yāti.

Even if the black mountain were ink, the ocean an inkpot, a branch of the wish-fulfilling tree a pen, the earth a writing leaf and if, using all these, the goddess of learning were to write for eternity, the limit of Your virtues would not be reached.

33. *Asura-sura-munīndrair-arcita-syendu-mauler*
Grathita-guṇa-mahimno-nirguṇa-syeśvarasya,
Sakala-gaṇa-variṣṭhaḥ puṣpadantā-bhidhāno
Rucira-malaghu-vṛttaiḥ stotra-metaccakāra.

The best of *gandharvas,* Pushpadanta by name, composed in great devotion this beautiful hymn to the Lord, who is worshipped by demons, gods, and the best of sages, whose praises have been sung, who has the moon on His forehead, and who is without attribute.

34. *Ahara-hara-navadyaṁ dhūrjaṭeḥ stotra-metat*
Paṭhati parama-bhaktyā śuddha-cittaḥ
pumānyaḥ,
Sa bhavati śivaloke rudra-tulya-stathā'tra
Pracura-tara-dhanāyuḥ putravān-kīrtimāṁśca.

If a person always reads this beautiful and elevating hymn to Shiva with a purified heart and great devotion, he will receive in this world abundant wealth, long life, many children, and fame. After death he will go to the abode of Shiva and become one with Him.

35. *Dīkṣā dānaṁ tapas-tīrthaṁ*
yoga-yāgā-dikāḥ kriyāḥ,
Mahimnaḥ stava-pāṭhasya
kalāṁ nārhanti ṣoḍaśīm.

Initiation into spiritual life, charities, austerities, pilgrimages, knowledge of scriptures, the performance of sacrificial rites—none of these gives even a sixteenth part of the merit that one gains by reciting this hymn on the greatness of Shiva.

36. *Āsamāpta-midaṁ stotraṁ*
puṇyaṁ gandharva-bhāṣitam,
Anau-pamyaṁ mano-hāri
śiva-mīśvara-varṇanam.

Thus ends this unparalleled sacred hymn composed by Pushpadanta, describing the glory of Shiva in fascinating detail.

37. *Mahe-śānnā-paro devo*
mahimno nāparā stutiḥ,
Agho-rānnā-paro mantro
nāsti tattvaṁ guroḥ param.

There is no god higher than Shiva. There is no hymn better than the hymn on the greatness of Shiva. There is no mantra more powerful than the name of Shiva. There is no higher knowledge than the true nature of the Guru.

38. *Kusuma-daśana-nāmā sarva-gandharva-rājaḥ*
Śiśu-śaśa-dhara-mauler-deva-devasya dāsaḥ,
Sa khalu nija-mahimno bhraṣṭa evāsya roṣāt
Stavana-midama-kārṣīd-divya-divyam mahimnaḥ.

The lord of *gandharvas,* Pushpadanta by name, is the servant of the god of gods, who has the crescent moon on His forehead. Having fallen from his glory due to the wrath of the Lord, incurred when he stepped on flowers used for His worship, he composed this very beautiful, uplifting hymn on the greatness of Shiva to regain His favor.

39. *Suravara-muni-pūjyaṁ svarga-mokṣaika-hetuṁ*
Paṭhati yadi manuṣyaḥ prāñ-jalir
nānya-cetāḥ,
Vrajati śiva-samīpaṁ kinnaraiḥ stūyamānaḥ
Stavana-midama-moghaṁ puṣpadanta-praṇītam.

If one recites with single-minded devotion and folded hands this unfailing hymn composed by Pushpadanta, which is adored by gods and the best of sages and which grants heaven and liberation, then, being worshipped by *kinnaras,* one goes to Shiva.

40. *Śrī-puṣpadanta-mukha-paṅkaja-nirgatena*
Stotreṇa kilbiṣa-hareṇa hara-priyeṇa,
Kaṇṭhas-thitena paṭhitena samā-hitena
Suprīṇito bhavati bhūta-patir-maheśaḥ.

If a person learns by heart, recites, or meditates on this hymn, which flowed from the lotus mouth of Pushpadanta, which destroys sins and is dear to Shiva, and which equally promotes the good of all, then Shiva, the lord of creation, becomes very pleased.

41. *Ityeṣā vāṅ-mayī pūjā*
śrī-macchaṅkara-pādayoḥ,
Arpitā tena deveśaḥ
prīyatāṁ me sadā-śivaḥ.

This hymnal worship is offered at the feet of Shiva. May the ever-propitious lord of gods be pleased with my action!

42. *Yadakṣaraṁ padaṁ bhraṣṭaṁ*
mātrā-hīnaṁ ca yad bhavet,
Tat-sarvaṁ kṣam-yatāṁ deva
prasīda para-meśvara.

If any letter or word has been left out, or if any letter has been mispronounced, please forgive me, O God, and be gracious.

43. *Om pūrṇamadaḥ pūrṇamidaṁ*
pūrṇāt pūrṇamudacyate,
Pūrṇasya pūrṇamādāya
pūrṇamevāvaśiṣyate.

Om. That is perfect. This is perfect. From the perfect springs the perfect. If the perfect is taken from the perfect, the perfect remains.

Om śāntiḥ śāntiḥ śāntiḥ.

Om. Peace! Peace! Peace!

ŚIVA MĀNASA PŪJĀ

Mental Worship of Shiva

1. *Ratnaiḥ kalpitamāsanaṁ himajalaiḥ*
   snānaṁ ca divyāmbaraṁ,
   Nānāratna-vibhūṣitaṁ mṛgamadā-
   modāṅkitaṁ candanam;
   Jātī-campaka-bilva-patra-racitaṁ
   puṣpaṁ ca dhūpaṁ tathā,
   Dīpaṁ deva dayānidhe paśupate
   hṛtkalpitaṁ gṛhyatām.

O ocean of mercy, O master of bound creatures, I have imagined a throne of precious stones for You, cool water for You to bathe in, divine robes adorned with many jewels, sandalwood paste mixed with musk to anoint Your body, jasmine and champaka flowers and bilva leaves, rare incense, and a shining flame. Accept all these which I have imagined in my heart for You, O God.

2. *Sauvarṇe nava-ratna-khaṇḍa-racite*
   pātre ghṛtaṁ pāyasaṁ,
   Bhakṣyaṁ pañcavidhaṁ payodadhiyutaṁ
   rambhā-phalaṁ pānakam;
   Śākānāma-yutaṁ jalaṁ rucikaraṁ
   karpūra-khaṇḍojjvalaṁ,
   Tāmbūlaṁ manasā mayā viracitaṁ
   bhaktyā prabho svīkuru.

Sweet rice in a golden bowl inlaid with the nine jewels, the five kinds of food made from milk and curd, bananas, vegetables, sweet water scented with camphor, and betel leaf — I have prepared all these in my mind with devotion. O Lord, please accept them.

3. *Chatraṁ cāmarayoryugaṁ vyajanakaṁ*
cādarśakaṁ nirmalaṁ,
Vīṇā-bheri-mṛdaṅgakāhalakalā
gītaṁ ca nṛtyaṁ tathā;
Sāṣṭāṅgaṁ praṇatiḥ stutirbahuvidhā
hyetatsamastaṁ mayā,
Saṅkalpena samarpitaṁ tava vibho
pūjāṁ gṛhāṇa prabho.

A canopy, two yak-tail whisks, a fan and a spotless mirror, a *vīna,* kettledrums, a *mridang* and a great drum, songs and dancing, full prostrations, and many kinds of hymns — all this I offer You in my imagination. O almighty Lord, accept this, my worship of You.

4. *Ātmā tvaṁ girijā matiḥ sahacarāḥ*
prāṇāh śarīraṁ gṛhaṁ,
Pūjā te viṣayopabhogaracanā
nidrā samādhisthitiḥ;
Sañcāraḥ padayoḥ pradakṣiṇavidhiḥ
stotrāṇi sarvā giro,
Yadyatkarma karomi tattadakhilaṁ
śambho tavārādhanam.

You are my Self; Pārvatī is my reason. My five *prānas* are Your attendants, my body is Your house, and all the pleasures of my senses are objects to use for Your worship. My sleep is Your state of *samādhi.* Wherever I walk I am walking around You, everything I say is in praise of You, everything I do is in devotion to You, O benevolent Lord.

5. *Karacaraṇakṛtaṁ vāk*
kāyajaṁ karmajaṁ vā,
Śravaṇanayanajaṁ vā
mānasaṁ vāparādham;
Vihitaṁ vihitaṁ vā
sarvametat kṣamasva,
Jaya jaya karuṇābdhe
śrīmahādeva śambho.

Whatever sins I have committed with my hands, feet, voice, body, actions, ears, eyes, or mind, whether prohibited by the scriptures or not, please forgive them all. Hail! Hail! O ocean of compassion! O great God! O benevolent Lord!

KUṆḌALINĪ STAVAḤ

Hymn to the Kundalinī

1. *Janmoddhāra-nirīkṣaṇīha taruṇī*
   vedādi-bījādimā,
   Nityaṁ cetasi bhāvyate bhuvi kadā
   sadvākya-sañcāriṇī;
   Māṁ pātu priya-dāsa-bhāvaka-padaṁ
   saṅghātaye śrīdharā,
   Dhātri! Tvaṁ svayam ādideva-vanitā
   dīnātidīnaṁ paśum.

The Kula Kundalinī is (always) looking (for opportunities) to redeem (Her devotees) from (the cycle of) birth (and death). She is ever young. She is the origin of the Vedas and other (scriptures) as well as the seed letters. In this world, yogīs apprehend Her through the mind. Sometimes She exists in the words of saints. Let that auspicious one protect me so that I may attain (divine) union. I consider myself to be Her beloved servant. O Mother, you are naturally the wife of that primordial God, whereas I am a bound soul, more wretched than the wretched.

2. *Raktābhāmṛta-candrikā lipimayī*
   sarpākṛtir nidritā,
   Jāgrat-kūrma-samāśritā bhagavati
   tvaṁ māṁ samālokaya;

Māṁsodgandha-kugandha-doṣa-jaḍitaṁ
vedādi-kāryānvitaṁ,
Svalpa-svāmala-candra-koṭi-kiraṇair
nityaṁ śarīraṁ kuru.

(The Kula Kundalinī) has a red luster. She is the nectarean moonlight. She is of the form of the letters. She has the shape of a serpent and is sleeping. O revered one, You who resort to the eyes as *kūrma prāna* during the waking state, look at me. My body has the defect of being filled with a foul stench, the odor rising from the flesh, and is always engaged in performing Vedic rituals. Make it (pure and) eternal with a small portion of Your millions of pure moonbeams.

3. *Siddhārthī nija-doṣavit sthalagatir*
vyājīyate vidyayā,
Kuṇḍalyā kula-mārga-mukta-nagarī-
māyā-kumārgaḥ śriyā;
Yadyevaṁ bhajati prabhāta-samaye
madhyāhna-kāle'thavā,
Nityaṁ yaḥ kula-kuṇḍalī-japa-padām-
bhojam sa siddho bhavet.

One who wants perfection and knows his own shortcomings becomes victorious while living on earth through the knowledge of Shrī Kundalinī. (Being freed from) the wrong path of *māyā,* (such a one reaches) the city of liberation through the path of Kula Kundalinī. If, during the time of early morning or at noontime, one regularly worships the lotus feet of the hymn of the Kula Kundalinī, one becomes a Siddha.

4. *Vāyvākāśa-caturdale'tivimale*
vāñcha-phalonmūlake,
Nityaṁ samprati nitya-deha-ghaṭitā
sāṅketitā bhāvitā;
Vidyā kuṇḍala-māninī sva-jananī
māyā kriyā bhāvyate,
Yaistaiḥ siddha-kulodbhavaiḥ praṇatibhiḥ
sat-stotrakaiḥ śambhubhiḥ.

O very pure one, who uproots the fruits of desires, yogīs meditate on You in the four-petaled (lotus of *mūlādhāra*), where the wind (of passion) and the space (of consciousness) exist. (There) they always rightly think of You as having the eternal symbolic form (of a serpent). Those who worship the self-respecting coiled one with prostrations and with the beneficent sacred hymns that originate from the clan of Siddhas become liberated. She is knowledge. She is Her own mother (self-born). She is *māyā* (the power of delusion) and *kriyā* (the power of action).

5. *Dhātā-śaṅkara-mohinī tribhuvana-*
chāyā-paṭodgāminī,
Saṁsārādi-mahā-sukha-praharaṇī
tatra sthitā yoginī;
Sarva-granthi-vibhedinī sva-bhujagā
sukṣmātisukṣmā parā,
Brahma-jñāna-vinodinī kula-kuṭī
vyāghātinī bhāvyate.

Remaining there (in the *mūlādhāra),* that yoginī infatuates (even) Brahmā and Shiva. She lifts the veil of the shadow of the three worlds, destroys (the seemingly) great happiness of worldly existence, and pierces all the (inner) knots. She Herself (assumes the form of) a serpent. She is subtler than the subtlest. She is the supreme one reveling in the knowledge of Brahman. She is conceived as the one who has *mūlādhāra* as Her house and who strikes at (worldly bondage).

6. *Vande śrī-kula-kuṇḍalīṁ trivalibhiḥ*
sāṅgaiḥ svayambhū-priyāṁ,
Prāviṣṭāmbara-māracitta-capalāṁ
bālā-balā-niṣkalām;
Yā devī paribhāti veda-vadanā
sambhāvanī tāpinī,
Iṣṭānāṁ śirasi svayambhu-vanitāṁ
sambhāvayāmi kriyām.

I bow to Shrī Kula Kundalinī. She is the beloved of the self-born one and surrounds Him (the Shivalingam, or representation of Shiva in the *mūlādhāra*) in three circles with all the members (of Her retinue). She enters the space *(sahasrāra)* and becomes active like the mind intoxicated with love. She is naive, defenseless, and complete. The Goddess, who shines with the Vedas as Her countenance, procures (everything for Her devotees) and burns (those who become averse to Her). I worship Her, the wife of the self-born one, who revels in the head *(sahasrāra)* with Her chosen one. She is the power of action.

7. *Vāṇī-koṭi-mṛdaṅga-nāda-madanā-*
niśreṇi-koṭi-dhvaniḥ,
Prāṇeśī rasa-rāśi-mūla-kamalol-
lāsaika-pūrṇānanā;
Āṣāḍhodbhava-megha-rāji-janita-
dhvāntānanā-sthāyinī,
Mātā sā paripātu sūkṣma-pathagā
māṁ yogināṁ śaṅkarī.

To hail Her arise innumerable sounds, such as the sound of drums (and other instruments), emanating from the words of millions of intoxicated devotees. She is the ruler of *prāna*. Her face, which is like a blooming lotus rooted in the ocean of delicious elixir, is filled only with joy. Her face is dark (like the darkness) produced by the multitude of clouds appearing in Āshādha (the month of rains). She is the support of all. Let that mother who travels the subtle path *(sushumnā)* protect me from all sides. She is beneficent to yogīs.

8. *Tvām āśritya narā vrajanti sahasā*
   vaikuṇṭha-kailāsayor,
   Ānandaika-vilāsinīṁ śaśiśatā-
   nandānanāṁ kāraṇām;
   Mātaḥ śrī-kula-kuṇḍalī-priya-kale!
   kālī-kaloddīpane!
   Tatsthānaṁ praṇamāmi bhadra-vanite!
   māmuddhara tvaṁ paśum.

O Mother, having resorted to You, people immediately go to Vaikuntha (the abode of Vishnu) and Kailāsa (the abode of Shiva). You sport only in bliss. Your face (manifests) the joy of hundreds of moons. You are the source (of everything). O Mother, O Shrī Kula Kundalinī, the beloved manifestation (of Shakti), O illuminator of the Kālī aspect (of Shakti), O good lady, I bow to that place *(mūlādhāra)*. You uplift me, a bound soul.

9. *Kuṇḍalī-śakti-mārgasthaḥ*
   stotrāṣṭaka-mahā-phalam,
   Yaḥ paṭhet prātarutthāya
   sa yogī bhavati dhruvam.

If one who is stationed on the path of Kundalinī Shakti, rising early in the morning, recites this hymn of eight verses, which gives great fruit, he certainly becomes a yogī.

10. *Kṣaṇādeva hi pāṭhena*
kavinātho bhaved iha,
Pavitraḥ kuṇḍalī-yogī
brahma-līno bhaven mahān.

By its recitation, indeed, one becomes in a moment a great poet in this world. A yogī practicing Kundalinī Yoga, becoming pure and great, becomes one with Brahman.

11. *Iti te kathitaṁ nātha!*
kuṇḍalī-komalaṁ stavam,
Etat stotra-prasādena
deveṣu guru-gīṣpatiḥ.

O Lord, thus I have related to you this beautiful hymn of Kundalinī. By the blessing of this hymn one becomes learned, like the Guru of the gods.

12. *Sarve devāḥ siddhi-yutā*
asyāḥ stotra-prasādataḥ,
Dvi-parārdhaṁ cirañjīvī
brahmā sarva-sureśvaraḥ.

By the blessings of Her hymn, all gods are endowed with powers. Brahmā (the creator), the lord of all gods, lives as long as two *parārdhas.*

BHAJA GOVINDAM

Worship Govinda

Refrain:
Bhaja govindaṁ bhaja govindaṁ,
Govindaṁ bhaja mūḍhamate.

Worship Govinda, worship Govinda, worship Govinda, ignorant man!

Samprāpte sannihite kāle,
Nahi nahi rakṣati ḍukṛñkaraṇe.
(Refrain)

When the time to go is near, the *dukriñkarane* (memorizing grammatical *sūtras)* will not protect you.

1. *Dinam-api rajanī sāyaṁ prātaḥ*
   śiśira-vasantau punarāyātaḥ,
   Kālaḥ krīḍati gacchatyāyus
   tadapi na muñcatyāśāvāyuḥ.
   (Refrain)

Day and night, evening and morning, winter and spring come again and again! Time rolls on, life is spent, yet the wind of desire does not leave him.

2. *Agre vahniḥ pṛṣṭhe bhānūḥ*
   ratrau cibuka-samarpita-jānuḥ,
   Kara-talabhikṣaḥ taru-talavāsas
   tadapi na muñcatyāśāpāśaḥ.
   (Refrain)

With a fire in front of him or the sun behind, huddled with his chin on his knees at night, he begs for food with only his bare hands. He lives under trees, yet the noose of desire does not leave him.

3. *Yāvad-vittopārjana-saktas*
   tāvannija-parivāro raktaḥ,
   Paścād dhāvati jarjara-dehe
   vārtāṁ pṛcchati ko'pi na gehe.
   (Refrain)

As long as he is able to earn money, his relatives remain attached to him. Later, when he dodders with his decrepit body, not even the people in his own house ask for news of him.

4. *Jaṭilo-muṇḍī luñcita-keśaḥ*
   kāṣāyāmbara-bahu-kṛta-veṣaḥ,
   Paśyannapi ca na paśyati muḍha
   udara-nimittaṁ bahu-kṛta-veṣaḥ.
   (Refrain)

With matted locks, a shaven head, or plucked hair, clad in many ways with ochre-dyed clothes, such fools can see but they do not see (the Truth). They are dressed in these different ways only for the sake of their stomachs.

5. *Bhagavadgītā kiñcidadhītā*
gaṅgā-jala-lava-kaṇikā pītā,
Sakṛdapi yasya murāri-samarcā
tasya yamaḥ kiṁ kurute carcām.
(Refrain)

If one has studied the *Bhagavad Gītā* even a little, or drunk the tiniest drop of water from the Gangā, or only once worshipped Murāri, what can Yama (the lord of death) say about him?

6. *Aṅgaṁ galitaṁ palitaṁ muṇḍaṁ*
daśanavihīnaṁ jātaṁ tuṇḍam,
Vṛddho yāti gṛhītvā daṇḍaṁ
tadapi na muñcatyāśāpiṇḍam.
(Refrain)

With body drained, hair turned white, and a toothless mouth, the old man walks supporting himself on a stick, yet the meat of desire does not leave him.

7. *Bālas-tāvat-krīḍā-saktas*
taruṇas-tāvat-taruṇī-raktaḥ,
Vṛddhas-tāvac-cintā-magnaḥ
tasmin brahmaṇi ko'pi na lagnaḥ.
(Refrain)

In childhood, one is engaged in play; in youth, one is attached to a young woman; in old age, one is burdened with anxiety; but no one is ever concerned with Brahman.

8. *Punarapi jananaṁ punarapi maraṇaṁ*
punarapi jananī-jaṭhare śayanam,

Iha saṁsāre bahu-dustāre
kṛpayā'pāre pāhi murāre.
(Refrain)

Born again, dying again, sleeping once again in a mother's belly — here in this endless ocean of *samsāra* (the world), which is difficult to cross, protect me by Your grace, O Murāri.

9. *Punarapi rajanī punarapi divasaḥ*
punarapi pakṣaḥ punarapi māsaḥ,
Punarapyayanaṁ punarapi varṣaṁ
tadapi na muñcatyāśāmarṣam.
(Refrain)

Another night, another day, another two weeks, another month, another half a year, and another year (all pass by), yet the passion of desire does not leave him.

10. *Vayasi gate kaḥ kāma-vikāraḥ*
śuṣke nīre kaḥ kāsāraḥ,
Naṣṭe dravye kaḥ parivāro
jñāte tattve kaḥ saṁsāraḥ.
(Refrain)

When youth is gone, where is passion? When the water dries up, can there be a lake? When wealth is lost, where are one's relatives? When the Truth is known, where is this world?

11. *Nārī-stana-bharanābhiniveśaṁ*
mithyā-māyā-mohāveśam,
Etan-māṁsa-vasādi-vikāraṁ
manasi vicāraya vāraṁ-vāram.
(Refrain)

A woman burdened with breasts and (the act of) entering below the navel are frenzied delusions brought on by deceitful Māyā. Reflect in your mind again and again that these are only modifications of flesh, fat, and so on.

12. *Kastvaṁ ko'haṁ kuta āyātaḥ*
kā me jananī ko me tātaḥ,
Iti paribhāvaya sarvam asāraṁ
viśvaṁ tyaktvā svapna-vicāram.
(Refrain)

Who are you? Who am I? Where have I come from? Who is my mother? Who is my father? In this way, think of everything as meaningless and renounce the world, knowing it to be just a dream.

13. *Geyaṁ gītā-nāma-sahasraṁ*
dhyeyaṁ śrīpati-rūpam ajasram,
Neyaṁ sajjana-saṅge cittaṁ
deyaṁ dīna-janāya ca vittam.
(Refrain)

Sing the *(Bhagavad) Gītā* and the *(Vishnu) Sahasranāma,* meditate unceasingly on the form of the Lord of Shrī (Vishnu), direct your mind to the company of saintly beings, and give money to needy people.

14. *Yāvajjīvo nivasati dehe*
kuśalaṁ tāvat pṛcchati gehe,
Gatavati vāyau dehāpāye
bhāryā bibhyati tasmin kāye.
(Refrain)

The people in his house ask after his well-being as long as life remains in the body, but when the breath has left his dead body, even his wife is afraid of his corpse.

15. *Sukhataḥ kriyate rāmābhogaḥ*
paścāddhanta śarīre rogaḥ,
Yadyapi loke maraṇaṁ śaraṇaṁ
tadapi na muñcati pāpācaraṇam.
(Refrain)

One enjoys a beautiful woman with pleasure, but look—afterward one's body becomes diseased. Although death is the only refuge in this world, still one does not give up sinful conduct.

16. *Rathyā-carpaṭa-viracita-kanthaḥ*
puṇyāpuṇya-vivarjita-panthaḥ,
Nāhaṁ na tvaṁ nāyaṁ lokas
tadapi kim-arthaṁ kriyate śokaḥ.
(Refrain)

With his clothes made of cast-off rags from along the road, a monk follows the path that is beyond merit and demerit. Neither you nor I nor this world exist, so why should he grieve?

17. *Kurute gaṅgā-sāgara-gamanaṁ*
vrata-paripālanam athavā dānam,
Jñāna-vihīne sarvam anena
muktir na bhavati janma-śatena.
(Refrain)

One may go to where the Gangā flows into the sea, observe vows, or give money in charity, yet by themselves these cannot release one without knowledge — even in a hundred lives.

GURUDEVA HAMĀRĀ PYĀRĀ

To Our Beloved Guru

Refrain:
Gurudeva hamārā pyārā
hai jīvana ko ādhāra. (2x)

Our Gurudeva is beloved to us! He is our life's support.

1. *Gurudeva kī hai apāra śakti*
   jīvana ko hai milatī sphūrti,
   Miṭe maila saba mana ke pār
   hai jīvana ko ādhāra.
   (Refrain)

Gurudeva's Shakti is limitless. We derive from him our life force, which removes all impurities from our minds. He is our life's support.

2. *Unako apanā jīvana jāno*
   tana mana dhana saba unako māno,
   Vo hī lagāve pār
   hai jīvana ko ādhāra.
   (Refrain)

Know him to be your own life. Consider him to be your body, mind, and wealth. He alone can take us across the ocean of this world. He is our life's support.

3. *Nityānanda śaraṇa jo jāve*
   bodha ujālā so hī pāve,
   Mukta hota hai niradhāra
   hai jīvana ko ādhāra.
   (Refrain)

Whoever seeks refuge in Nityānanda obtains the light of knowledge; he becomes free and has no need for other support. He is our life's support.

4. *Muktānanda kahai saba āo*
   śrīgurudeva nām nita gāo, (2x)
   Ho bhavabhaya se pār
   hai jīvana ko ādhāra.
   (Refrain)

Muktānanda says, "Come, all of you. Always sing the name of Shrī Gurudeva, and overcome the fear of the cycle of birth and death." He is our life's support.

NIRVĀṆAṢAṬKAM

Six Stanzas on Salvation

1. *Mano-buddhyahaṅkāra-cittāni nāhaṁ*
Na ca śrotra-jihve na ca ghrāna-netre,
Na ca vyoma bhūmir na tejo na vāyuś
Cidānanda-rūpaḥ śivo'haṁ śivo'ham.

I am neither the conscious nor the unconscious mind, neither intelligence nor ego, neither the ears nor the tongue nor the senses of smell and sight, neither ether nor air nor fire nor water nor earth. I am consciousness and bliss. I am Shiva! I am Shiva!

2. *Na ca prāṇa-sañjño na vai pañca-vāyur*
Na vā sapta-dhātur na vā pañca-kośaḥ,
Na vāk-pāṇi-pādaṁ na copasthapāyū
Cidānanda-rūpaḥ śivo'haṁ śivo'ham.

I am neither the *prāna* nor the five vital airs, neither the seven body components nor the five sheaths, neither speech nor hands nor feet nor anus nor sex organ. I am consciousness and bliss. I am Shiva! I am Shiva!

3. *Na me dveṣarāgau na me lobhamohau*
Mado naiva me naiva mātsarya-bhāvaḥ,
Na dharmo na cārtho na kāmo na mokṣaś
Cidānanda-rūpaḥ śivo'haṁ śivo'ham.

Neither aversion nor attachment, neither avarice nor delusion, neither arrogance nor the feeling of jealousy, at all, neither righteousness nor wealth nor pleasure are mine. I am consciousness and bliss. I am Shiva! I am Shiva!

4. *Na puṇyaṁ na pāpaṁ na saukhyaṁ na duḥkhaṁ*
Na mantro na tīrthaṁ na vedā na yajñāḥ,
Ahaṁ bhojanaṁ naiva bhojyaṁ na bhoktā
Cidānanda-rūpaḥ śivo'haṁ śivo'ham.

I am neither virtue nor vice, neither pleasure nor pain, neither mantra nor sacred place, neither Vedas nor sacrifices. I am neither the food nor the eater nor the act of eating. I am consciousness and bliss. I am Shiva! I am Shiva!

5. *Na mṛtyur na śaṅkā na me jāti-bhedaḥ*
Pitā naiva me naiva mātā ca janma,
Na bandhur na mitraṁ gurur naiva śiṣyaś
Cidānanda-rūpaḥ śivo'haṁ śivo'ham.

Neither death nor doubt nor caste distinction, neither father nor mother nor even birth are mine, at all. I am neither brother nor friend, neither Guru nor disciple, indeed. I am consciousness and bliss. I am Shiva! I am Shiva!

6. *Ahaṁ nirvikalpo nirākāra-rūpo*
Vibhutvācca sarvatra sarvendriyāṇām,
Na cāsaṅgataṁ naiva muktir na meyaś
Cidānanda-rūpaḥ śivo'haṁ śivo'ham.

I am without thought, without form. I am all-pervasive, I am everywhere, yet I am beyond all senses. I am neither detachment nor salvation nor anything that could be measured. I am consciousness and bliss. I am Shiva! I am Shiva!

Sadgurunāth Mahārāj kī Jay.

Hail to the true Guru.

ĀRATĪ LĪJO

Accept Our Worship

Refrain:
Āratī lījo aja avināśi
Pūraṇa nityānanda prakāśī
Pūraṇa muktānanda prakāśī (2x)
Āratī lījo

Accept our worship, O unbegotten, imperishable, O perfect Nityānanda, radiating light; O perfect Muktānanda, radiating light.

Nabha aur dharaṇī āratī thālā
Candra sūraja doū dīpa ujālā (2x)
Agara candana saba dhūpa birāje (2x)
Jhūlā merana cāvara tarana rāśī
(Refrain)

The sky and the earth are your *āratī* platters; the moon and sun your bright flames; the agara and sandal trees your incense powder; Mount Meru your swing; and the branches of trees your whisks.

Phūla vanaspati haĩ ye sārī
Sātõ sāgara jala kī jhārī (2x)
Gagana anāhata bājẽ bāje (2x)
Gāje rāga ḍare yama pāśī
(Refrain)

All the plants offer their blooms; the seven seas pour their currents of water; drums beat in the spaces of the heart; melodious sounds resound. Death cowers in fright in your noose.

Cāra prakāra ke anna gopālā
Soī tero bhoga rasālā (2x)
Loka caturdiśa mandira tero (2x)
Ghaṭa ghaṭa āsana svayaṁ vikāsī
(Refrain)

The four kinds of food, O Gopālā, offer their sweet nectars to you. The fourteen worlds are your temples. Every heart rolls itself out as a mat for you, O self-luminous one.

Mahāvākya vedana ke jo haĩ
So tero caraṇāmṛta so haĩ (2x)
Sadguru pujārī deo caraṇāmṛta (2x)
Pīyẽ narīnara bandha vināśī
(Refrain)

The great statements of the Vedas are the sacred water of your feet, O Sadguru. O holy priest, grant us the sacred water of your feet. Let men and women sip it, O destroyer of bondage.

ŚRĪ MAHĀLAKṢMYAṢṬAKAM

Hymn to Mahālakshmī

Śrī gurubhyo namaḥ,
Śrī lābh śrī śubh śrī gaṇeśāya namaḥ.
Mahālakṣmyaṣṭakaṁ stotram.

Salutations to the Guru; salutations to Ganesha, the auspicious one.

1. *Namaste'stu mahāmāye*
   śrīpīṭhe surapūjite,
   Śaṅkha-cakra-gadā-haste
   mahālakṣmi namo'stute.

Salutations to you, Mahāmāyā, abode of fortune, worshipped by gods, wielder of conch and mace, Mahālakshmī, obeisance to you.

2. *Namaste garuḍārūḍhe*
   kolāsura-bhayaṅkari,
   Sarva-pāpa-hare devi
   mahālakṣmi namo'stute.

Salutations, O rider of Garuda, terror of the demon Kola, remover of sins, beloved goddess, Mahālakshmī, obeisance to you.

3. *Sarvajñe sarvavarade*
   sarva-duṣṭa-bhayaṅkari,
   Sarva-duḥkha-hare devi
   mahālakṣmi namo'stute.

Knower of all, giver of all boons, a terror to the wicked, remover of all sorrows, beloved goddess, Mahālakshmī, obeisance to you.

4. *Siddhi-buddhi-prade devi*
   bhukti-mukti-pradāyini,
   Mantra-mūrte sadā devi
   mahālakṣmi namo'stute.

Bestower of intelligence and success, O goddess, bestower of worldly enjoyment and liberation, with the mantra always as your form, goddess Mahālakshmī, obeisance to you.

5. *Ādyanta-rahite devi*
   ādyaśakti maheśvari,
   Yogaje yogasambhūte
   mahālakṣmi namo'stute.

Without beginning or end, O goddess, primordial energy, great mistress born of yoga, Mahālakshmī, obeisance to you.

6. *Sthūla-sūkṣma-maharaudre*
   mahaśakti mahodare,
   Mahā-pāpa-hare devi
   mahālakṣmi namo'stute.

In the form of the gross and subtle bodies, Rudra's Shakti, source of all, remover of great sins, beloved goddess, Mahālakshmī, obeisance to you.

7. *Padmāsana-sthite devi*
parabrahma-svarūpiṇi,
Parameśi jagan-mātar
mahālakṣmi namo'stute.

Seated on a lotus, O goddess, true Self of the supreme Brahman, O supreme mistress, universal mother, Mahālakshmī, obeisance to you.

8. *Śvetāmbaradhare devi*
nānālaṅkāra-bhūṣite,
Jagat-sthite jagan-mātar
mahālakṣmi namo'stute.

Clad in white apparel, O goddess, bedecked with a variety of jewels, supporter of the universe, universal mother, Mahālakshmī, obeisance to you.

9. *Mahālakṣmyaṣṭakaṁ stotraṁ*
yaḥ paṭhed bhaktimān naraḥ,
Sarva-siddhim avāpnoti
rājyaṁ prāpnoti sarvadā.

This hymn to the great goddess of wealth, if read with devotion, will bestow all success, will grant all worldly position.

10. *Eka-kāle paṭhen nityaṁ*
mahā-pāpa-vināśanam,
Dvi-kālaṁ yaḥ paṭhen nityaṁ
dhana-dhānya-samanvitaḥ.

If always read once a day, great sins will be destroyed. If always read twice a day, wealth and prosperity will ensue.

11. *Tri-kālaṁ yaḥ paṭhen nityaṁ*
mahāśatru-vināśanam,
Mahālakṣmīr bhaven nityaṁ
prasannā varadā śubhā.

If always read three times a day, the great enemy (ego) will be destroyed. Mahālakshmī will be ever pleased with that auspicious one.

Sadgurunāth Mahārāj kī Jay!
Hail the true Guru!

Appendix

1. How to Pronounce the Mantras

In developing good Sanskrit pronunciation there are three main elements to understand and practice: the time taken to pronounce each letter, the placement of the tongue, and the aspiration — the amount of air that accompanies each letter.

Time is measured in *mātrās,* one *mātrā* being approximately the amount of time it takes to snap the fingers. Generally, this system of measurement applies only to vowels, since consonants do not usually appear without an accompanying vowel sound. Long vowels are held for two *mātrās,* short vowels for one *mātrā,* and consonants for one-half *mātrā.* (See Pronunciation Guide that follows). The distinction between long and short vowels is essential because, in Sanskrit, an alternation in the length of one letter can change the meaning of a word entirely.

Tongue position is equally important, because the placement of the tongue changes the pronunciation of a letter, and this can also change the meaning of a word. The tongue positions for the various letters correspond to a gradual movement of the sound from deep within the back of the throat outward to the lips. There are three types of letters in the Sanskrit alphabet: (1) consonants, which are divided into five classes (*vargas*); (2) vowels; and (3) letters that are neither vowels nor consonants. The tongue positions for these are as follows:

CONSONANTS	
Guttural	Sounds and tongue are at back of throat
Palatal	Front of tongue is placed rather flatly against front of roof of mouth
Lingual	Tip of tongue curls up to touch middle of roof of mouth
Dental	Tip of tongue touches back of teeth, almost coming out between them
Labial	Sounds are made with the lips
VOWELS	Normal tongue placement
OTHER LETTERS	See Pronunciation Guide

In Sanskrit it is very important to distinguish consciously between aspirated and unaspirated consonants, because the distinction often creates changes in the meanings of words. In English, however, unvoiced consonants (t, p, and k) are often unconsciously aspirated. Therefore, for Westerners nonaspiration of these consonants in Sanskrit is often difficult to apply. With careful listening and practice, however, one can make the correct distinction between the aspirated and unaspirated letters in the Sanskrit alphabet. The following examples in English illustrate this distinction:

The "b" in "about" is unaspirated, but the "t" in the same word is aspirated.

The "p" in "apple" is generally unaspirated, whereas the "p" in "put" is aspirated.

The "c" in "cake" is aspirated, whereas the "k" is fairly unaspirated.

The first "k" in the imperative "kick it" is aspirated, but the second one is not.

The main thing to understand here is that, in Sanskrit, an unaspirated consonant is one that is followed by no air at all, whereas an aspirated consonant is usually followed by about the same amount of air as a regular English unvoiced consonant and is produced very naturally.

2. Pronunciation Guide

Letter	English equivalent	English sound	Time (number of *matras*)	Aspiration	Other information
VOWELS					
a	short "a"	c*u*p, b*u*tter	1	no	
ā	"ah"	f*a*ther, c*a*lm	2	no	
i	short "i"	b*i*t, s*i*p	1	no	
ī	"e"	sc*e*ne, h*ea*t	2	no	
u	—	h*oo*k, p*u*t	1	no	
ū	long "u"	l*oo*p, sc*oo*p	2	no	
e	long "a"	f*a*ce, s*a*ve	2	no	
ai	short "a" + short "i"	—	2	no	neither "ay" nor long "i," but in between the two
o	"o"	ph*o*ne, p*o*ke	2	no	
au	short "a" + "u"	—	2	no	neither "ow" nor long "o," but in between the two
SEMI-VOWELS					
aḥ	—	—	1½ or 3	yes	in the middle of a sentence the vowel is followed by a slight aspiration, but at the end of a sentence the vowel is repeated lightly, preceded by the aspiration
aṁ	—	—	1½	no	vowel is finished with a nasal sound in between "m" and "n"
ṛ	—	—	1	no	a rolled "r" followed by a vowel sound in between "i" and "u"
ṝ	—	—	2	no	a rolled "r" followed by a "u"
CONSONANTS					
ka *varga* (gutturals)					
ka	—	kic*k* it	½	no	
kha	"k"	*kook*	½	yes	
ga	"g"	*g*ood, *G*od	½	no	
gha	—	do*gh*ouse	½	yes	
ṅa	"ng"	ri*ng*ing	½	no	

Letter	English equivalent	English sound	Time (number of *matras*)	Aspiration	Other information
ca *varga* (palatals)					
ca	—	su*ch*	½	no	su*ch* is a good approximation, but the sound is actually softer and not aspirated
cha	"ch"	*ch*uck, *ch*ew	½	yes	
ja	—	ju*dg*e	½	no	again, the sound is somewhat softer than this
jha	—	he*dgeh*og, sle*dgeh*ammer	½	yes	
ña	—	ca*ny*on, o*ni*on	½	no	
ṭa *varga* (linguals) (important: tip of tongue curls up to roof of mouth for all these letters)					
ṭa	—	pu*t*	½	no	
ṭha	"t"	boa*th*ouse	½	yes	
ḍa	"d"	*d*id	½	no	
ḍha	—	roa*dh*ouse	½	yes	
ṇa	"rna"	My*rna*	½	no	
ta *varga* (dentals) (important: tip of tongue is on teeth for all these letters)					
ta	—	s*t*op	½	no	
tha	—	an*th*ill	½	yes	*not* as "th" in the English word "thing"
da	—	mi*dd*le	½	no	
dha	—	—	½	yes	
na	—	s*n*ake	½	no	
pa *varga* (labials)					
pa	—	a*p*ple	½	no	
pha	"p"	loo*ph*ole	½	yes	*not* pronounced "f"
ba	"b"	a*b*out	½	no	
bha	—	a*bh*or	½	yes	
ma	"m"	*m*ayor	½	no	
SEMI-CONSONANTS					
ya	"y"	*y*es, *y*et	½	no	
ra	—	—	½	no	rolled once lightly
va	—	—	½	no	between "v" and "w"; "v" may be used for convenience without being incorrect
la	"l"	*l*ayer	½	no	more like a French or Spanish "l"

Letter	English equivalent	English sound	Time (number of *matras*)	Aspiration	Other information
SIBILANTS					
sa	"s"	*s*aw	½	no	dental
śa	"sh"	*sh*oot	½	no	palatal
ṣa	—	—	½	no	like "sh" but with the tongue placed as for a lingual
DOUBLE CONSONANT					
kṣa	—	auc*ti*on	1	no	like "ksha" but with tongue placed as for a lingual
ASPIRATE					
ha	"h"	*h*at	½	yes	

3. Guide to Diacritical Marks

EXAMPLE	EXPLANATION
ā, ī	A line over a vowel indicates that it is long. This means that it has a distinctive sound and is held for 2 *mātrās*. (Note: not all long vowels have this mark; see the Pronunciation Guide for details.)
ḍ, ṇ	A dot under a letter (except "h" or "r") means that the letter is pronounced with the tip of the tongue curling up to touch the roof of the mouth; i.e., it is lingual.
ã, ẽ	*Sadguru kī Āratī* and the first part of the morning and evening *Āratī* are in Marathi rather than Sanskrit or Hindi, and for this reason a tilde (~) over a vowel is used to indicate a nasal sound made at the back of the throat with the mouth open; the sound is similar to the ending of "hu*nh*" or the nasalized vowels in French.

EXAMPLE	EXPLANATION
ñ	An "n" with a tilde is pronounced "nya."
jñ	When preceded by a "j," the same "n" is pronounced "jnya." (Note: "gnya" or "dnya" may also be used.)
aḥ	An "h" with a dot under it is pronounced as a slight aspiration. However, at the end of a sentence the vowel preceding the ḥ is pronounced again but is held for only half the length of time, making the whole syllable either 1½ or 3 *mātrās* long. For example, in *tasmai śrigurave namaḥ,* the last word is pronounced *namaha;* the first "a" in the syllable *aha* is held for 1 *mātrā* and the second for ½ *mātrā.*
ṛ	A dot under an "r" indicates that the "r" is rolled and pronounced with a vowel sound in between "i" and "u."
ṅ	A dot over an "n" means that it is pronounced "ng."
ṁ	A dot over an "m" means that the final sound is an indeterminate nasal somewhere in between "m" and "n." A pronunciation of "m" would not be incorrect.
ś	An "s" with an acute accent is pronounced "sh."

4. Conjuncts

Consonants written together (jj, cc, cch, nn, tt, etc.) are called conjuncts. The letter written twice is pronounced as a single sound and is held for 1 *mātrā.* In this connection, it is important to remember that in Sanksrit every letter is pronounced; there are no silent letters.